HOW TO OVERCOME NERVOUS TENSION
AND SPEAK WELL IN PUBLIC

HOW TO OVERCOME NERVOUS TENSION

AND

SPEAK WELL IN PUBLIC

by

Alfred Tack

CEDAR

An imprint of William Heinemann Ltd

Published by Cedar Books
an imprint of
William Heinemann Limited
Michelin House, 81 Fulham Road, London SW3 6RB
LONDON   MELBOURNE   AUCKLAND
Copyright © 1955 by Alfred Tack
All rights reserved
First published as a Cedar Book 1974
Seventh impression 1988

0 434 11106 6

Printed in Great Britain by
Richard Clay Ltd, Bungay, Suffolk

FOR MY BROTHER GEORGE, WITH GRATEFUL
THANKS FOR HIS ENCOURAGEMENT, HELP AND
ADVICE

Contents

CHAPTER I

Speaking in Public is Easy

"Don't worry about it," said my brother George. "You probably need a break. Go away for a week."

I shook my head. I knew that I did not need a holiday—I enjoyed my work too much for that. "I'm not asking for sympathy," I replied, "and I don't want a holiday. Probably I'm a little stale, that's all. Or do you think that my voice is not as strong as it used to be?"

George smiled, and as he walked towards the door leading to the platform, to begin his next lecture, he said, "I'll keep them awake, don't worry."

But I was worried. For the first time in more than twenty years of lecturing and making speeches, a member of the audience had gone to sleep—at least, it was the first time I had noticed it. Normally, that wouldn't have been so bad, but it was during a lecture which, previously, had always been highly successful. I had to blame myself. Returning to my office I decided to forget the whole thing.

One hour later George returned looking very glum and said, "He must be Rip Van Winkle himself! He slept through the whole of my session too."

The solution to the mystery of the sleeping man came soon afterwards. We asked him to join us for tea, and tactfully mentioned that it is usually considered upsetting by speakers if a member of the audience dozes off without apparent cause. He told us that he was slightly deaf, and that he was probably the only slightly deaf man in the world who could hear better when he shut his eyes tightly than he could with them open.

This is just one incident in a lifetime of talking from platforms, from behind tableclothed tables, from stages, and from one hundred and one other places from which people expect public speakers to speak. Everything has happened to me, and I have made every conceivable mistake. This book has been written to stop these things happening to you, or, if they do happen to you, to enable you to know how to deal with them.

To get the best out of it imagine that I am writing for you alone. Forget about everyone else who may read it. When I write YOU, I mean you who are reading now.

First of all the heading of this chapter may have irritated you. *Speaking in public easy indeed! If it were, no-one would want to buy your book!*

That's a fair comment. But here is a fact for you to think about: Most people can converse quite well when amongst friends in their home, in a saloon bar, or in a club (for example, do you remember the way you talked about that holiday, or the road accident you saw; or the way you expressed yourself when you were 'all steamed up' about what had happened to you at the office?). Why, then, shouldn't they be able to speak in the same manner to a larger circle of people?

Perhaps *your* answer to that question is as follows:

"In the first place I am not all that good as a conversationalist. Secondly, I am not certain about my voice being heard in a large room or hall; and thirdly, I am scared stiff at the very idea."

You admit, then, that you can converse reasonably well, but you feel that there is a lot of room for improvement. Good! Here is my promise:

If you apply the lessons taught in this book you will become a good conversationalist, which means that you will be able to speak well in public. Your worries regarding your voice will largely disappear, and you won't be frightened to talk to a gathering of people, however large it may be. A little nervous, yes. But that's good for you. Some people call that excitement (and it can disappear almost at will), but scared— never!

What was that you thought, sir? This doesn't apply to you because you do speak in public and you are only reading this book to improve your technique?

This is the way it can help you: Most of us are average in many things because we have picked up our knowledge as we went along and have never studied fundamentals. This applies to sport as much as to public speaking. For example, one of my colleagues was a very fine tennis player. He became Junior Champion of Great Britain, and also did well at Wimbledon. Why is it that to-day, although he hardly plays at all, he can take on most club players who have taught themselves, and usually beat them? His answer is, "Once you know the fundamentals of each stroke you may lose a game but you will never play really badly."

Once you know the fundamental techniques of speaking in public, you can never make a bad speech.

You still don't think it is easy? I'll let you into a secret: there has been more nonsense written and talked about public speaking than almost any other subject. Why? Because many teachers set out to make a man or woman an accomplished orator. But you don't want to become another Demosthenes or Abraham Lincoln. You want to be able to stand on your own feet, full of confidence, and make a satisfying speech for yourself and your audience.

NO EXAMPLES

You will not find this book cluttered up with five thousand funny stories, ten thousand quotations and dozens of speeches made by great speakers of the present or past. It would be an easy way of filling up the book, but it wouldn't help you. The use of quotations will be dealt with later. My advice to you about joke books is to avoid them. Great speeches, like great books of poems and fiction, are something you enjoy reading or you don't. Because you don't like Shakespeare doesn't mean that you cannot speak well. I have found that students who enjoy reading the great works read them anyway, and don't need extracts in a book of this kind.

At one time we did our best to persuade students to study the masters and to read the classics. We were rarely able to achieve the desired result. To force yourself to study examples of brilliant oratory will not assist you. All that will happen is that you will become bored with the subject, and we rarely succeed at anything which does not interest us. I am always being reprimanded by my more scholarly friends for making this statement, but there is nothing like training thousands of would-be public speakers to learn what helps a man, and what does not.

HE'S A BORN SPEAKER

In fairy stories the fairy queen waves her magic wand over the forehead of the new-born babe, and for ever after he or she is proof against the wiles of witchcraft.

The day I see a fairy queen do the same for a new arrival to enable him to become a great speaker I shall believe that speakers are born with a gift of oratory. I shall also believe in fairies.

Most good speakers achieve success because at some time in their lives they have wanted to speak. They began, and they kept on speaking. The great majority, however, devote a lot of their time to perfecting themselves in the art of public speaking.

The fellow with the 'gift of the gab' is rarely a good speaker. He is not sincere enough. Any average man or woman with an average vocabulary can make himself or herself a first-class technician. We have had men through our classes who blushed every time they spoke, and kept mumbling something about not being born speakers. Others have been too conscious of a poor vocabulary, or have been too worried because of a voice with a squeak in it. These men have become good speakers. They have made themselves successful by being willing to learn from others, and by application of what they were taught.

Forgive me if that sounds boastful, but how else can I prove to you that the 'born speaker' idea is a myth?

NO JOB

He was young and excited. He had, at long last, received a tentative offer of a good position abroad.

It was the position he had yearned for. The only snag was the fact that he had to appear before a selection board.

He appeared. He failed to impress them. He knew exactly what he wanted to say before the meeting, but on being confronted by five stern-looking executives he had dried up. When he undried he said the wrong things. He failed to obtain the position, and for a time he was most miserable.

How do I know how he failed? Because he was me. I had been selling for about three years, but even that experience didn't help me to stand up and make out a case for myself.

I wonder how many times that kind of thing has happened to other people. The selection panel was probably right as far as I was concerned, but this need not always be the case. Long experience in advising companies has taught me that sometimes a good man has been passed over because of his inability to express his opinions in a proper manner. Some good speakers are, of course, windbags. But, usually, an executive sees through that pretty quickly. The choice, however, is not always between a windbag and a silent man. Sometimes it is between a first-rate silent man and quite a good fellow who has been able to marshal his facts and present them well. It is under these conditions that the job often goes to the latter.

Therefore, *the ability to speak well is one of the major factors in achieving success*.

FOR SUCCESSFUL MEN TOO

Many executives become quite upset at the thought of having to speak in public. Because for so many years business was easy to obtain (after all, the sellers' market lasted for a long time) the ability to speak well was not so important. That is no longer the case, however. Executives have to travel abroad to speak to other executives. They have to serve on various committees. They have to address their staff. They have to talk at dinners and luncheons.

Some avoid these business essentials, but it makes them unhappy, although they try, often, to mislead themselves by thinking that there is no need for them to speak well for the benefit of their businesses. They are unhappy because they are never really able to play the game of make-believe with themselves. No good executive likes to feel that he is not doing everything he should do for his concern. Some executives are not popular with their staff only because they cannot express themselves effectively. How can an executive be expected to handle people well when he cannot talk to them properly? I have often advised managing directors to talk regularly to their employees—to put the workers into the picture regarding the company's activities. This can help considerably in preventing labour disturbances. The majority of them make excuses, the usual one being, "They wouldn't appreciate it." The real reason in most cases is the inability of the managing director to express himself well in public.

ENJOYMENT AS WELL

The ability to speak well helps people in all walks of life to achieve success, and is an essential quality for an executive. True, some men who reach the top are *men of few words*, but most of these men have used plenty of words while climbing the ladder.

Even if we leave out the success factor in public speaking, it is still something worth learning and applying. Praise and honest appreciation are something which most of us need. The majority of people also like helping others, if they can. You may have held back from going on to a sports committee. Possibly you asked for your name to be deleted from the list of candidates for a position of honour. The reason may well have been your lack of confidence in your conversational ability.

Those who take part in local government, charitable organisations or committees formed to help others, in dramatics, sport, or anything else, enjoy themselves immensely. They often complain that they 'don't know why they do it', but they do it because they like doing it. They thrive on the honest appreciation they get for the work they do so well. Some would be happier still if they had made a more careful study of public speaking.

Another point—the good public speaker is usually a good conversationalist, and a good conversationalist (not someone who just wants to be in the limelight and monopolise the conversation) is welcome everywhere.

Public speaking, then, is essential for: executives, politicians, barristers, local government officials, the clergy, leaders in every sphere of life, teachers and club officials.

Public speaking will always help: those who have to communicate ideas, salesmen, officers in the Services, those interested in social welfare, actors and actresses (very few of these are good public speakers), and those interested in any kind of committee work.

ENTHUSIASM

By now you will be anxious to get on to the first lesson. But don't be in too much of a hurry. I want to impress you further with what the ability to speak well in public can do for you. I am doing this because I am enthusiastic about it, and I want you to feel the same.

There is a great deal that you have to do, and only if I am able to inspire enthusiasm in you can I be sure that you will begin to carry out our teachings right away.

Learning to speak well has helped many people:

To Overcome Self-consciousness and Shyness. Perhaps you don't suffer in this way, but thousands do. Sometimes this doesn't keep them quiet, it turns them into blusterers. In any event, if it can be eradicated it must be beneficial.

To Marshal Thoughts in an Orderly Manner. To be able to think clearly under all conditions is a fine asset.

To Develop Latent Ability. Many people have latent ability which is only latent because they are unable to express their thoughts clearly and with conviction.

To Increase Income. One example of this: How many people have good ideas which they have been unable to turn to their advantage because they could not present their ideas in a convincing manner?

To Develop Poise. Public speaking breeds confidence, which helps to develop poise.

To Increase Their Circle of Friends. The person who can talk on many matters in an interesting manner is always a welcome visitor. And as I have already mentioned, it also helps people to play their part in communal life, and to address an audience of twenty or two hundred.

IT'S EASY

As I have already told you, if you are enthusiastic you won't find speaking in public hard to master. But there is one proviso. That is: YOU MUST LIKE HELPING OTHERS.

Now that may seem strange to you, but nine times out of ten a speech is bad because the speaker is a selfish man. I don't mean that he is normally selfish in his everyday life, I am only referring to public speaking. Many a speaker thinks of himself first, last and all the time, forgetting his audience. He wants to speak well to satisfy himself. He wants all the applause and the pats on the back. He blames the audience when his speech falls flat or when that wonderful story doesn't raise a laugh.

Of course, he may not blame the audience. He may think that he was perfect anyway, just because the chairman has told him so afterwards.

If you are asked to make a speech, you must first decide whether you can do good. If you cannot, then don't make the speech.

Here are the questions you must ask yourself:

Can I teach them something?
Can I inspire them?
Can I arouse sympathy?
Can I entertain them?
Can I persuade them to do something for the good of the community?
Can I pay tribute sincerely to a person, and so make the audience feel that I am truly representing their feelings?
Can I impart some information which will help them?

This may sound old-fashioned, but a speaker must feel that he has a message for his audience. It is only when he has this sense of urgency that he makes a really good speech. I shall do my best to see that you are able to deliver that message, confident that you will not let yourself down.

CHAPTER II

No Butterflies . . .

THERE is a glazed look about his eyes, but this is not through drinking too many cocktails. He has only had a small glass of sherry, and he feels that another may steady him.

"Thank you waiter," he says, accepting a glass.

"Darling," his wife's voice seems strangely distant, "I shouldn't have another if I were you. You know it upsets your liver."

"You have another, John"—a friend's voice this time. "Put you right for your speech."

A spasm passes through his body. He is conscious of the fact that he is perspiring freely. He makes a feeble joke and swallows. There are voices . . . voices . . . voices . . .

"Hello, John, meet my boss . . ."

"Hello, John, how are you?"

"John, may I introduce Bill Smythe, he's my guest . . ."

Voices . . . voices . . . voices . . .

"Darling," it's his wife's voice this time. "You must excuse me for a moment. I must go across and have a word with the Honourable Mrs. Wiggins."

Suddenly he is conscious that his wife has left his side.

"Waiter!" he shouts—and his voice seems very loud. "Waiter, a double whisky please, quickly."

Down goes the double . . .

"Waiter, another please."

Down goes another. All to no effect, he is still coldly sober.

"You're not having another, are you, dear?" His wife has returned.

"No," this time his voice sounds hollow. "I'm just holding this for Bill."

Nobody laughs.

At last it is time for dinner.

Food—drinks—chatter. Food—chatter—drinks. Gossip—jokes—food. It's over. The toastmaster is about to announce the loyal toast. Soon it will be his turn. His stomach revolves. He stands up. He sits down.

Notes! Notes—where are they? Glasses—where are his glasses? Somebody is whispering in his ear. His heart is thumping. He feels more than slightly sick, and there is a strange weakness in his knees.

What's that fellow calling out? Why, it's his own name! They're applauding! Oh dear, it's arrived at last. He stands up. All eyes are upon him . . .

Many a man has felt like that. In fact, we asked a hundred men who attended our Courses to describe their feelings before making a speech. These men have spoken on odd occasions for years, they were not novices, but their feelings ranged from almost petrification to an unfeeling numbness which caused their thoughts to be hazy and jumbled. Only three out of the hundred told us that they felt a harmless kind of nervous excitement. This, then, is a major problem in public speaking.

IS COURAGE THE ANSWER?

Many ways have been suggested to enable a speaker to get rid of those butterflies. A politician, who is

recognised now as a first-class speaker, told me that he
nearly gave up his career because of the hours of
endless misery he had to endure, especially during
electioneering times. He was told by an Elder States-
man in the party to have courage and to have faith in
himself, but this advice didn't help.

I well remember a much-decorated naval officer,
who had shown not the slightest concern when his
ship was under intense enemy fire, asking for a glass
of water before I took him on to a platform, because he
felt a little queer. He was in such a high state of nerves
that he didn't even ask for gin in it.

Men of courage are greatly to be admired. But
courage doesn't help them to overcome pre-platform
nerves. I have sometimes been told that it is far better
to be a man of action that a spouter. But why shouldn't
a man have both these assets? A spouter need not
necessarily be spineless; and the man of action need
not be dumb. In point of fact, to-day, some of the
world's greatest do-ers are also wonderful speakers.

In days gone by explorers read papers on their
return from the wilds, and read them before learned
bodies. Nowadays these men and women return and
thrill all of us with their exploits, by talks on television
and wireless. They benefit financially. We benefit by
becoming armchair explorers for a while.

Faith in oneself must go the same way as courage.
Both faith and courage will get a man on to the platform, whereas without these attributes he might back
out at the last minute, but they won't stop the jitters.

No, "Hold your head high", "Have courage",
"Believe in yourself"—this kind of advice won't
help.

HOW ABOUT AUTO-SUGGESTION?

Does auto-suggestion solve the problem? Well, it can help. The power of suggestion is great indeed—but there is a snag. You may have been telling yourself that you have only to visualise yourself doing something confidently, and that will come to pass. This, to a limited extent, is a psychological fundamental. It is based on the power of the subconscious mind. You fail, the argument goes on, because you see yourself as a failure. This is so implanted in your inner mind that at the crucial moment the failure picture will be forced into your mind, and you will make the mistakes that you have previously visualised.

If that is so, then the obvious conclusion is that we have only to visualise ourselves not making mistakes, and then the success images will come to us when we need them.

All of this can happen, provided you know how to use auto-suggestion, which is a form of self-hypnosis. It can do a power of good, but here's the drawback—Coué, who pioneered auto-suggestion, made it clear that it is sometimes necessary to have outside help to enable a person to get into the frame of mind to accept suggestions. He made another point: If we try to achieve something too quickly this way, the opposite to what is intended may occur. This, put simply, means that if you visualise yourself speaking calmly and well but you know that you don't expect this to happen, the failure thought will come to your mind automatically, and this negates the success thoughts. Even when thinking of simple sentences for the purpose of auto-suggestion, he tells us that one sentence must follow another without pause, to avoid negative thoughts breaking in.

This is a very deep subject, and from my experience I would say that it is only a great help to the people who have received some instruction in auto-suggestion. For nine people out of ten, the advice to think of themselves as a success to enable them to lose their tension and to speak confidently does not help at all.

There is one way in which it can help, but that we shall deal with later.

DEEP BREATHING

We are told that if we are nervous we have only to breathe deeply and the nervousness will disappear. Extra oxygen taken into our lungs will achieve this.

Of course it helps. It helps in dozens of situations, but not always in public speaking.

If a speaker is not too nervous he should breathe normally. And if he is highly nervous, then deep breaths before he speaks will give him just that amount of time to become almost overwhelmed with the immensity of the occasion.

A stage artist told me that when he first appeared on television he was extremely nervous. He tried the deep-breathing technique, and as he did so he suddenly realised that millions were looking at him. He was hardly able to get the first few words of his talk out at all.

We have found that it is better for a speaker to begin talking the second he is on his feet. Only the professional speaker can take his time before commencing.

CONFIDENCE THROUGH KNOWLEDGE

A thorough understanding of the subject about which one is going to speak is, obviously, an essential. But it isn't the complete answer to nervous tension. You must have heard dozens of speeches by experts in their own subjects, whose talks have been spoiled by nervousness which tended to accentuate their mannerisms. In fact, at our Courses we invariably have many men and women arriving who know their subjects thoroughly, but still that quaking feeling has persisted.

For all that, many speakers would lose quite a lot of their nervousness if they were to take more time over the preparation of their speeches. If these speakers know their subjects well, what, then, are their main fears? They are the same as the fears of those who are conscious of the fact that they have not mastered their subject as well as they should have done.

(a) Fear of failure.
(b) Fear of looking foolish.
(c) Fear of breakdown.

The fear of failure can be eased by complete preparation.

The fear of looking foolish is partly brought about by incomplete preparation, but more generally by inexperience in speaking.

The fear of breakdown is the most common fear. It doesn't help a great deal to tell the would-be speaker that it rarely occurs. However, one thing which invariably does cheer up those who come to us is that these three fears are common to practically everyone in the room. It is surprising how much this fact helps. When we suffer from something we always think that we are the only one to suffer in this way. When we realise that our neighbour feels exactly the same as we do, then we don't feel quite so bad about it.

Another thing that we encourage is for a speaker to talk about his failings to someone else. We have what we call a Clinic for this purpose, and time and again we have immediately restored confidence merely by telling a speaker that what has happened to him has happened to so many others.

Let us face the fact—it is impossible for anyone first entering the field of public speaking not to make some mistakes due to nervousness. Bernard Shaw once said, *I became a good speaker as other men become good skaters—by making a fool of myself until I got used to it.*

There isn't any need to go as far as that, because there is a main cause for speaking nerves, which can be cured. Before going into this, however, here are some of the ways in which a speaker can do something about his jitters.

(a) Use notes correctly. This will be dealt with fully later, but let me say now that the incorrect use of notes adds to tension.

(b) When nervous, look at a member of the audience and speak to him as if you were having a conversation with him.

(c) If you forget a part of your speech and you haven't any notes, recapitulate. Generally, the forgotten passage will come to your mind when you do this.

DO REMEMBER THIS

Every speaker feels nervous before a speech. We call it nervous excitement and this can actually help the speaker. It is only when it causes dryness of the mouth, which makes speaking so difficult that it results in a person mumbling and stuttering, that it must be dealt with. I am mentioning this because, even when we rid you of your nerves, you will still feel that excited feeling before a speech.

WHAT WE LEARNED

Years of training public speakers has taught us that there are only two ways of tackling this problem of nerves. One is a short-term policy which helps every speaker immediately, and the other is a complete cure, which takes a few months to achieve.

Many years ago we believed, in common with all teachers of public speaking, that the one thing to avoid at all costs was allowing a student to make a mistake, which might result in his losing confidence in himself. Courses were spread over twenty weeks, so that we could gradually get the student to speak more and more. We became most worried for fear that a student might feel even the slightest bit uncomfortable on the platform. Let him start off with one sentence was our plan. Then two sentences . . . After the fifth or sixth week he could speak for a minute, and so it went on. We had to save embarrassment at all costs, otherwise we felt it would live with the student for ever, and he would never be able to speak in public.

We couldn't have been more wrong. We gave them

confidence all right. Confidence to speak in front of the same men in whose company they had been speaking for some twenty weeks. We had developed well-protected parrots, who were no use away from their own circle of friends. Some told us that all their nervousness returned when speaking amongst strangers. Their worries of breakdowns and failures had not left them, just because the Course had been prolonged.

We decided to switch right over. All the experts said we were wrong. Time has proved us right.

What does a trapeze artist do if he falls into the safety net? He gets right back and does the same part of his act again.

What happens when a comedian fails in a show? Does he give up the stage? Not likely! He fights all the harder to get into another show, to prove that he is successful.

Are salesmen coddled along? Of course they're not! I have known salesmen to leave a buyer red-faced, shaken, almost with tears in their eyes. That was when they started. Most of them went on selling.

If the gradual theory had been correct, then these men, who are, in fact, public speakers before small audiences, would have to have preparation spread over months and months before they were able even to face a buyer. Now we know that a would-be speaker should begin making speeches as quickly as he can. In our lecture room we start right away by bringing a student on to the platform, where the lecturer begins a conversation with him. The lecturer continues the conversation but he moves away from the platform, and the student goes on talking. Soon he finds himself alone talking to the lecturer, who is at the back of the hall. Then he continues on his own—and all this in front of strange faces. Mistakes are made, of course. Some may feel uncomfortable, but they are so very glad of this afterwards.

We tell them to make all their mistakes in the lecture room before strangers, and they won't worry then nearly so much when facing an audience.

Far from affecting their confidence in themselves, this new method of teaching actually creates confidence.

The short-term policy, then, to overcome speaking nerves is to have those nerves and get over them quickly.

Obviously, everyone cannot take a course in public speaking, so here is the answer to the problem: it is a long-term policy, but it will help you to overcome this trouble in about six months.

THE RIGHT WAY TO OVERCOME NERVOUS TENSION

It all began many years ago. When teaching salesmen to sell, we discovered that we had to consider the buyers' reaction to salesmen selling them something that they needed although they did not realise this need. Under these conditions we found that the buyers became tense. They only relaxed when, and if, they decided to buy. This tension on the part of the buyers often arose because of over-selling on the part of the salesmen, who were themselves far too tense. By teaching them how to relax, we found they were able to sell in an easy conversational manner, which in itself enabled the buyers also to relax.

During these courses we taught salesmen and sales managers public speaking, because we felt that those in the selling field should be able to speak before an audience. It was soon obvious to us that once nervous tension disappeared through relaxation selling became easier and pre-speaking nerves became non-existent. The answer to nervousness, then, is really simple:

When you can relax properly you cannot feel nervous.

Although we have only taught the art of relaxing to help speakers and salesmen, the results in other directions have given us much happiness. We have had hundreds of letters from ex-students telling us that relaxing has cured them of stammering, blushing, insomnia, stomach troubles and all kinds of nervous ailments. Only a few days before writing this chapter of the book, a director of a commercial company called to see me, to tell me that for the first time in ten years he is free of migraine headaches.

All this, as I have said, makes teaching the art of relaxation well worth while. However, we teach it because, after a great deal of trial and error, we have found it to be the only complete answer to the problem of speakers' nerves. If it also helps you in other directions—so much the better.

This is how we explain the cause of tension: A student is asked if he would find it difficult to repeat the nursery rhyme *Little Jack Horner* while still seated in his chair. He usually answers that it would present no difficulty. He is then asked if he would still feel the same if invited to come up on to the platform and repeat the same rhyme. Invariably he replies that he might feel a little uncomfortable about that. The next question is, "There are five thousand people at the Royal Albert Hall and I should like you to go there and recite the nursery rhyme in front of them. Now how would you feel about that?"

The student admits that he would be shaking at the knees at the thought of doing any such thing.

But why? The words of the rhyme are well known. Why should the student find it easy to repeat them in the body of the lecture room, and almost impossible from the platform of the Royal Albert Hall?

The answer was given to me by a doctor, much learned in all things of the mind and body; he said that the muscles of our body automatically tense themselves whenever the unusual is expected of us. The cycle of events operates in this manner: On being asked to come to the platform to recite, the student's muscles tense. Fear messages rush to the brain, the brain returns these messages to the muscles, which become even more tense. Tense muscles form poisons, which travel through the blood-stream. These cloud the mind, and the thoughts become still more muddled. More messages to the muscles—more tenseness, more muddle, and so on. These are not the exact words used by my friend the doctor, but, roughly, they explain his meaning.

Now, perhaps, you can see why some speakers cannot even read their notes. Their thoughts become so jumbled through tenseness that they are unable to think properly.

The answer should be clear to you: If first by practice, and later automatically, your muscles can be relaxed, pre-speech nerves will go for ever.

Just think of that. No if's or maybe's, but a complete cure. However, this won't happen by itself. You have got to do something about it.

If you do, you will find that before many months have passed, so soon as you are faced with any situation which normally would bring tenseness followed by nervousness, your muscles will automatically relax themselves, and no tenseness will be felt.

In the previous chapter I mentioned auto-suggestion and told you that it was not easy to apply. That is because it is axiomatic of auto-suggestion that a person must be in a completely relaxed state before it can even begin to be applied.

First learn to relax, and then auto-suggestion may well be of greater help to you.

HOW TO DO IT

When first we realised that relaxing was the answer to many problems—to relieve nervous tension is something necessary for so many people to-day—I tried all methods to master this apparently simple art. At one time I thought it was essential for the mind to be an absolute blank before a person could relax, and I spent considerable time with my eyes closed, thinking of black velvet.

Yet again, on one occasion I was informed that it was impossible to relax unless the eyeballs were rolled upwards. This I tried as well. I must have rolled them so high that they almost reached my scalp, but all this did for me was to concentrate my mind on what I was doing, which in itself, brought tension.

I could not find the answer when I attempted to

achieve results quickly. I tried with my feet resting on walls, while my head was resting on the ground because I heard that this was a good position for relaxing. Another method was to use sloping boards, with a pillow placed beneath limbs to give more comfort and get the body into the right position for relaxing—but still no results.

It took me a long time to find the solution, and when I found it, it was so simple. It is one which has now been practised by our students for a long time, and which they have found easy to master. We call it *the minute technique*.

THE MINUTE TECHNIQUE

If you try to relax for half an hour or even for ten minutes, you will probably fail. You will almost certainly do this unless you have practised relaxing for some time. When doctors advise their patients to take time off and relax for half an hour every day, they are giving excellent advice, but few can carry it out. The average person tells himself to relax, and no sooner is he sitting down in a comfortable position than all the worries that are at the back of his mind come to the fore—and that's the end of relaxing for that day.

Relaxing must become a habit, and the way to make it a habit is to start in such a small way that you need devote so little time to it that it doesn't become a strain—it doesn't worry you, and it doesn't set up negative thoughts.

Now most people can concentrate their mind on something for a minute at a time, and that's all you have to think about, to begin with. But before you

come to that we have to make it simpler still. You
couldn't think of your whole body for a minute at a
time. But you could think of one part of your body
quite easily.

If I ask you now to think of your hand for a few
seconds you could do that. In the first place, then, we
have to simplify matters, by dividing the body up into
several parts—seven, in fact. When we have done that
we find it easy to think of any of these parts when we
wish to. Here they are:

> Your left-arm muscles.
> Your right-arm muscles.
> Your left-leg muscles.
> Your right-leg muscles.
> Your stomach and chest muscles.
> Your back muscles.
> Your face muscles.

Now think, for a moment, of your left arm. That's
easy enough, isn't it? You will have to think about
that for just a minute, a little later. Before you
concentrate on your muscles, however, you have to
remember two words. There isn't anything original
about these words. They have been used for many,
many years. If you tell yourself to relax it doesn't seem
to have much effect, but if you tell a muscle, or a part
of your body, to "Let go" then, after a while, the
muscles do just that—they let themselves go. We use
it as a standard expression when anybody is tense. We
often say, "For goodness' sake let yourself go!"

So far, then, you have to remember only seven parts
of your body and the two words, "Let go".

Now to commence the minute technique: Start it

to-night when you go to bed—or right now if you wish, and if you are on your own. For one minute only—and it doesn't matter if it is a little less—concentrate all your thoughts on the muscles of your left arm. Don't worry about the rest of your body—the left arm only. Now tense the muscles until it almost hurts. Then quietly say to your muscles, "Let go". Say the word "let" as you breathe in; "go" as you breathe out. Keep that up for one minute, and then forget the whole thing.

Next day, when you have a little spare time (perhaps after lunch, or while you are waiting to see someone), concentrate on that left arm again, and once more tell the muscles to let go. Continue this for seven days. You will know when the muscles are properly relaxed, because you will get a warm, tingling feeling in them— and this is a very comfortable feeling.

Few people can even relax an arm muscle without practice. You can prove it to yourself, if you wish, by asking a friend to relax and then lift his left arm high into the air. You will rarely find that it will drop when you let it go. He will hold it in the air, or else bring it down slowly. This means that he is not relaxing at all, because if he were, as you let go of his left arm it would flop to his side automatically, and that is what you have to achieve.

The second week

The second week you must concentrate all your thoughts on your right arm. Think about it for one minute at a time, for two or three times a day and when you go to bed. Forget all about your left arm. You will find that it will automatically relax itself, but don't worry about it.

The third week

The third week you will carry out the same procedure with your left leg.

To do this you must be sitting down or lying in bed. When sitting, don't cross your legs, place your feet flat on the ground.

The fourth week

Now you will concentrate on your right leg, forgetting all about your arms and your left leg.

The fifth week

This time you think about your stomach and chest. Once again, don't forget to tense your muscles first, and then let go.

The sixth week

Now it's the turn for your back muscles.

The seventh week

It is your facial muscles this time. Your teeth must not be clenched. There must be no wrinkles on your forehead.

Now a warning: Don't hurry! Remember this is a long-term policy. Better be a first-class speaker in six months than a bad one all your life, through overlooking this relaxation fundamental. I would rather you spent two weeks on each part of your body than only five or six days on each part.

DON'T HURRY—DON'T HURRY—DON'T HURRY

That's the secret.

Assuming that you make good progress, you will be

relaxing completely in seven weeks. For the following two or three months you can concentrate all your thoughts on your whole body, and let all your muscles go. Remember, only for a minute at a time. After that period has elapsed you will discover, as many others have done already, that you will be relaxing automatically, which was your aim from the beginning.

Only after six months have passed should you try to relax for longer than a minute at a time.

Now in which way is this technique different from others? It is this: We try to make relaxing an unconscious habit. It is only of value to the public speaker when, as tensions are about to begin, they are immediately counteracted by the relaxing of the muscles. That will happen to you if you carry out this advice for six to nine months.

As one student said to me, the lesson on relaxing is worth everything, even if one did not aim to speak in public.

But you do—that is why you are reading this book. For your own sake, then, make the effort. It is the one certain answer to a difficult problem. Don't expect miracles the first week or so. You will not notice very much difference for quite a while. Then it all happens quickly. The secret of this success is that there must be no preparation, no ritual. Here are the rules you require: Remember them in this order.

1. Remember seven parts of the body—
    the left arm
    the right arm
    the left leg
    the right leg

        the stomach and chest
        the back
        the face

2. Remember "Let go".
3. Start with the left arm. Tense it. Tell the muscles to "Let go" and keep repeating this for one minute. Start to-night when you go to bed. Then repeat it two or three times a day.
4. Concentrate only on your left arm for the first seven to ten days.
5. After seven to ten days, concentrate on your right arm, and *forget your left arm*. Carry on for seven to ten days.
6. Concentrate in turn on the remaining five parts of your body—seven to ten days for each part.
7. After two or three months, carry out the same "Let go" procedure while dealing with your whole body.
8. After six months, keep on practising regularly to relax, but increase the time to from two to five minutes for each period.
9. You must keep up the short daily relaxing exercises until your muscles respond automatically at the least sign of tension.

And now for some don'ts:

Don't tense your muscles more than once in each session. You only tense them in the first place to enable you to realise the fact that you are subsequently relaxing your muscles.

Don't try to relax your whole body while sitting down. Rest your arms on your uncrossed legs and concentrate on relaxing your arms and legs only.

Don't wrinkle your forehead, or close your eyelids tightly, or your mouth tightly, when relaxing your facial muscles.

And that is all you need to know to enable you to make relaxing a habit.

Sometimes students tell me after a session that they are deeply interested in relaxing and can I tell them more about it in private. On other occasions I have been asked to write a book on our *minute technique for relaxation*.

The answer to the student is that if I knew of any more help that I could give him, I should give it during the session. So far as the book is concerned, I couldn't fill one, without padding and still more padding.

Relaxation is *not* difficult. You can make it difficult if you want to, but why do that? The reason why this system has been so successful is because it is easy to master. You can concentrate easily for a minute, and by constantly doing this two or three times a day the habit becomes a part of you.

DO IT

Now it is up to you. If you carry out the advice given in this chapter you will overcome tension and you *won't be able* to feel highly nervous before that big speech. You will relax automatically, and you will be left with a pleasant feeling of excitement.

All speakers have that. It means that they are getting ready to give of their best.

Master relaxation and you will never spoil a speech through nervousness.

Butterflies? Now you know what to do about them!

CHAPTER III

Seeing Ourselves . . . !

GEORGE said, "You lean. And what is worse, you lean both ways. In fact you go backwards and forwards so often that you are beginning to look like one of those toy Kellys."

"Thank you," I replied. "But in the first place there is not a vestige of truth in your remarks; and secondly, if I do lean a little, that's far better than your collar act."

"And what," asked George, mustering a handful of dignity, "is my collar act?"

"It begins," I answered, "with the action of putting one finger in the front of your collar, just behind the tie space. You then do a giraffe act, and stretch your neck, at the same time waggling it sideways. While doing this, you tug at your collar."

"But that," said George, "only happens when I have a tight collar."

"Then," I replied, "you must always be wearing tight collars."

"My giraffe waggle," said George, "is still preferable to your backward and forward pendulum movements."

The discussion ran on these lines for some little while. It was all well meant. We have been together in business for some thirty years, and haven't had a serious quarrel yet. This has been a great help, because we have been able to criticise each other without starting a row and we have in this way become con-

SEEING OURSELVES . . . !

scious of our mannerisms. As you know, everyone
hates criticism and most of us fight back when criticised. We rarely believe that the criticism is fair. It is
for this reason that most of us have so many minor
faults, which we could easily put right if we could find
them out for ourselves.

Let's face it—however hard we try we shall still fall
a great deal short of perfection. But if we keep perfection as a goal, we shall make much better public
speakers, and possibly better citizens.

Here is a truism: Mannerisms on the platform or
behind a dining-table can ruin a good speech. It is
because of this that I am dealing with this subject early
in the book.

Most teachers of public speaking treat mannerisms
as of minor importance. They work on the assumption
that there is nothing so important as the gradual
building up of the speech. That is true, provided that
an irritating manner does not ruin the whole presentation. You simply cannot listen to a speaker when your
eyes and thoughts are concentrated on whether or not
he is going to blow his nose for the twentieth time.

Do not, then, hurry through this chapter, but think
carefully about it while reading it. In fact, don't read
the next chapter at all until you have checked up on
yourself. The difficulty we have in dealing with this
subject is that very few people believe they have any
mannerisms. I didn't believe I leaned. My brother was
oblivious of the fact that he played with his collar.

If we are conscious of these mannerisms we sometimes make ourselves believe that they are assets. One
student, with wildly tousled hair, thought he looked
like a famous film star. It took us a long time to make

him realise that he really looked as if he had just come
out of a swimming pool, and the action of continually
brushing back his hair with his hand could be most
irritating to an audience.

We always have difficulty in this respect in dealing
with the I-want-to-learn-it-all-quickly businessman.
He doesn't want to know anything about this 'manner-
ism nonsense'. The strange thing is that this type of
man invariably has mannerisms which he should try
to eradicate. I do hope that I have persuaded you not
to treat this matter lightly.

What was that you thought? Was it: *You can't be
right, Mr. Tack. What about old X? He looks like nothing
on earth, and he's always scratching his head. But what a
wonderful speaker!*

We often hear that thought expressed. The answer
is that there are always exceptions to every rule. They
are, however, so few and far between in public speaking that you will be wiser not to make yourself believe
that you are one of those exceptions. Remember, bad
speaking habits are much more difficult to cure once
you have started making a few speeches.

Now let us begin with the audience's reactions to the
speaker. They run on these lines:

> First, they *look* at him.
> Next, they *listen* to him.
> And finally, they *notice his actions*.

They begin to look at the speaker from the moment
he walks on to the platform. If he is going to speak
after a dinner has finished, then they begin to watch
him for some minutes before his speech commences.
If for any reason they don't like his attitude or his

manner, they can easily be biased against him before his speech commences.

WALKING ON

How are you going to walk on to the platform? Don't do it in any of these ways:

The Slinker

He does just that. He slinks on to the platform as if guilty of something. Perhaps he does feel guilty about the disappointment his audience may feel after listening to him.

The Absent-minded

He looks as if he has arrived at the wrong place. First he sits in the wrong chair. When finally seated correctly, he gazes round the room as if he is not quite certain what it is all about.

The Pained

He looks thoroughly upset, and gives the impression that the whole thing is a complete bore.

The Strutter

He appears to be so cocksure of himself that he immediately arouses antagonism.

The Jitterer

He seems to be so nervous that we all begin to feel nervous for him long before he starts to speak.

The right way to walk on to the platform is as if you had walked into the house of a great friend, whom you hadn't seen for some time. Look pleased to see the committee. Look as though you are glad to meet the audience, and if you will forgive the cliché, walk on with a purposeful air.

AT A TABLE

If you are speaking after a luncheon or dinner, then remember these don'ts:

Don't be a *wiper*

He is the speaker who, just before he rises to speak, dabs at his mouth with his napkin and then, as if told by his wife that he still has a few crumbs left on his lips, he dabs again. Sometimes he even gives a fresh dab as he stands up, and a final one as he beams at the guests.

Don't be a *gulper*

You know the gulper, of course. Seconds before rising he gives the appearance of a foreign legionnaire in the desert, who has found an oasis. He takes a wild swig of wine or water, and is still gulping as he rises to his feet. We think he is just going to begin his speech, when he has another gulp.

Don't be a *leaper*

The leaper leaps. It is as if the toastmaster had let off a squib, or an American guest had given him the hot foot, which is brought about by inserting a lighted match into the shoe. He leaps into the air, and the effect on the audience is quite startling.

Don't be a *Chain-and-Ball speaker*

Yes, he looks as though he is held down by a chain, it seems such an effort for him to get to his feet.

The right way? You know when your turn to speak will come—you know quite a few minutes beforehand. Wipe your mouth in good time, and have your final drink at leisure. Push back your chair so that you won't hit the table as you stand up, and then get to your feet as if you were welcoming an old friend.

THE HANDS

I know a most accomplished speaker who won for himself the nickname of Napoleon, because during most of his speeches he would stand with one arm bent and his hand inserted in the opening of his waistcoat. He told me that the habit had started years previously, when he had not known what to do with his hands while speaking. For some time he folded his arms, but that became too uncomfortable, and so he adopted, unconsciously, the other attitude.

That is an extreme case, but the number of speakers who do not seem to know what to do with their hands is surprising. There they go, into pockets, out of pockets, straight down the seams of the sides of the trousers, then back into pockets . . . Now upstairs into the armholes of the waistcoat. Then down again . . . And so it goes on.

There is no one solution to this problem. It is caused by a speaker not learning the fundamentals of his job. If he did he would first by habit, and then unconsciously, do the right thing with his hands. The right answer is *to know what to do with your hands, and to be able to forget them.*

WHAT TO DO

If it comes naturally to you to gesture, why then, that is the answer to what to do with your hands. From time to time you will move your hands to line up with what you are saying. Between times, you will forget them.

If a speaker does not find gestures come naturally to him, then he must try to do something about it. I have found that when the majority of would-be speakers attempt to use their hands, the result is most artificial. They are conscious of them, and by obviously trying to put matters right they make things far worse.

The true answer to this problem, once more, is relaxing. When that has been mastered, everything else follows naturally. Why? Because relaxation means that you are able to forget yourself. I know of no other simple way of dealing with this problem, and do please remember that we have tried every technique. Practising gesturing, dramatising your movements, a little emotionalism—possibly they all help, but only in a small way. Often they make a speaker stilted. If you want to stand in front of a mirror throwing your arms about, do so. Probably the exercise will be good for you, anyway. Far better to relax. Then what happens? As you speak, your hands help to picture some of your phrases. Your actions will help to prove your strong feelings about one or two of the points you are raising, and when you come to that stirring part of the speech with which you hope to arouse the audience, they will be more stirred because they will be able to SEE that you are excited about it yourself. No, gestures must come naturally, or not at all.

Try to explain to someone what a spiral staircase looks like, or how to knot a tie, and you will see what I mean. Your arm and hand movements then will be quite natural.

When you become a relaxed speaker you will find that sometimes your hands are by your sides, sometimes in your pockets. You won't care where they are, because you will not be conscious of them.

If you are still worried about your hands during the time that you take to master relaxation, then the best thing to do is to let your arms and hands hang loosely by your sides. That in itself will help you to relax a little.

LOOK RIGHT

Many a time I have heard speakers say, "I'm not putting myself out for them," or, "They can take me as I am or do the other thing."

These are the men who take little interest in their appearance. It is a kind of complex with them. It is as if they have a grudge against the audience. This, of course, hardly applies to after-dinner speakers, but it does apply to many visitors to clubs, societies, etc.

Your appearance *does* mean something. It gives a man just that little bit extra which is such a great help in winning an audience over. Tweed jackets and flannels and a pipe may be all right if you want to put over a couldn't-care-less act. If you are conscientious, and don't like this attitude, then you must realise that dress means a lot. The vast majority of first-class speakers do take great care to make sure that they look right.

Before going on to the platform, do remove those bulky things, pipes, wallets, etc., from the side pockets of your jacket. Do see that your tie fits properly into the collar space. If it is too low, or way across to one side, someone in the audience will lose what you are saying because he or she will want to come up and straighten your tie.

Brush your clothes—wait a minute. Why? Because you who are reading now may be a business executive, and you may look upon these things as fundamentals for children. Well, sir, I can only say that the biggest offenders in this respect are not the up-and-coming youngsters, but business executives.

Here is the best way of tackling this question: Ask your wife if what I have written applies to you. If it does, then do something about it from haircut to shoeshine. If it doesn't—well, you haven't wasted much time reading these few lines, have you?

MANNERISMS

We all have mannerisms. Most of them are harmless enough. It is only when they are repeated too often that they are apt to become irritating to others. Here are the most common mannerisms of speakers, which you will do well to avoid:

The Leaner

I did that, you will remember. Don't do it! I have stopped now—at least, I hope I have. Anyway, because I know that it is a fault, I can stop myself im-

mediately it starts. You can do the same. Don't lean—
don't sway. It makes people giddy.

The Fidget

This man badly needs to learn how to relax. He
cannot keep still. First he plays with an ashtray, then
he twirls a glass, and you watch to see if he will twirl
it right off the table. Then he steers things. His fore-
finger is on the table, making circles. You have the
idea that some salt has been spilt, and he is busy trying
to build a salt castle. You crane your neck to see.
What was that he said? You didn't hear? A pity, it
was something good! Well, he shouldn't have gone on
stirring. The fidget is never still—but then how could
he be? He is a fidget. No, not a born fidget. He
made himself like that, and he can cure himself if he
wants to.

The Puller

This speaker is continually pulling at his nose as if
it offended him. How did it all start? I have a suspicion
that the nose-puller started his act quite young. A film
star, possibly, did it just before he put the sixty-four
dollar question to a witness, which won him the
applause of jury, judge and spectators. It made him
look so thoughtful, so wise . . . And so another nose-
puller is made.

Don't do it, or if you do have to—if you think it
makes you look like Gregory Peck or someone—do it
only once.

The Armpit-Rester

You must have seen him at work. His jacket is
pulled back to show an expanse of waistcoat and up

into each corner where there are armholes, he sticks his thumbs. The fingers spread out like a fan, and so he stands in all his pompous glory.

Don't do it. It doesn't make you look important. Usually, all it draws attention to is an increasing girth.

The N.B. and C.

This is an abbreviation for the nose-blower and cougher. He seems to have a very heavy cold. Every few minutes he either blows, coughs, or clears his throat. It is most irritating to the audience, and most frightening to a hypochondriac if he should happen to be sitting in the front row.

The Scratcher

Like the nose-puller he feels that a careful scratch denotes thoughtfulness. But scratching is catching, and if he keeps it up he is likely to have the whole audience scratching themselves before he has finished.

First he scratches the side of his face, then his chin. Next comes the side again, and so on. Please don't scratch.

The Watcher

This speaker gives you the impression that he has a train to catch. He keeps looking at his watch.

It wouldn't be so bad if he were doing it because of his determination to keep to time. Sometimes he does say, "I have just five minutes more," and after ten minutes have passed he is apt to look again and tell you that he has just three minutes to tell you . . . You are likely to become a watcher yourself if this goes on for long.

Keep an eye on these mannerisms—no, not the other fellow's, I mean *yours*.

PETS

Besides our mannerisms we all have pet phrases which we trot out at regular intervals. Try to avoid repeating the same phrase or remark several times during a speech. For example:

> The point is . . .
> To put it plainly . . .
> As I was saying . . .
> That reminds me . . .
> Well . . .

You have the idea now. Check up on yourself, and try to cut down on all repetitive phrases.

> Finally, do watch out for
> ahh's
> mmm's
> err's

We all do it—the reason doesn't matter. There is hardly a speaker who doesn't ahh, mmm or err at some time or another. Do keep them to a minimum, however. Say one ahh, two mmm's and two err's during a twenty-minute speech and no-one will mind very much.

Do, please, think carefully about your mannerisms. They may not matter a great deal in your everyday life, although perhaps they do. They matter a great deal, however, to anyone who wants to make a success as a public speaker.

CHAPTER IV

Does It Apply To Me?

THE first night is over. The star returns to her dressing-room. The audience has not been too responsive. In the flower-filled room are gathered friends and friendly enemies.

"Darling, you were wonderful!"

"My dear, it will run for ever."

"I was so touched in the second act I cried."

"They should do something about the claque. I am sure X paid them to make a noise, but you needn't worry about them. Everyone else loved it."

"It's a smash hit."

And so on.

Disillusion comes next morning when the critics have their say.

She was miscast.

If it runs three nights it will be two too many.

I nearly cried during the second act—from exhaustion.

The claque in the gallery were right—they were entitled to their money back.

And so on.

What a game of make-believe is played in dressing-rooms and night clubs after first nights. A famous star once said, "I go straight home after a first night. I speak to no-one. Then I'm not so disappointed next morning if the criticisms are bad."

Much the same applies to speakers, except that they have no newspaper critics to put them right. It would be a good thing for all of us if we had sterner criticism.

No, we usually receive cries of acclamation like this:
"Good show, old man!"
"By Jove, you were good!"
"Just what they wanted."
"First class."
"Congratulations!"
And other similar remarks.

These well-meant expressions are voiced by the chairman, the chairman's wife and a few others at the top table. If criticism were allowed, maybe this is what the critics would say next day:

A poor presentation.

A terrible experience.

He went on and on—so boring.

He should never be allowed to speak, except within a closed room when he is on his own.

You see, as no-one tells us the truth, we mislead ourselves into thinking that we are good—and we often go on making speeches and boring people for years and years.

At a recent dinner I attended, the main speaker mumbled for one hour, when he was due to speak for twenty minutes. Everyone around me complained. I am quite sure, however, that when that speaker sat down the chairman, out of politeness, said to him. "Well done!"

Others must have made similar remarks, judging from the self-satisfied look on his face.

This, then, is another problem which must be solved. If others flatter us out of kindness we can only put matters right if we do a little hard thinking about ourselves. But you have to think objectively about yourself, and that is very, very difficult.

We always find it very hard at our Courses to convince those attending that what we have to teach applies to them. They are ready to absorb all that we have to say about speech-building and note-making, and how to present the speech, but as soon as we begin to lecture about some of the faults of individual speakers, we can *see* the effect. Those present take sidelong glances at their neighbours. How they pity them! Of course, it is the neighbour who has all the faults!

We ask them to use the *Does-it-apply-to-me?* formula. Throughout the whole Course they must keep asking themselves if what we teach applies to them, and not to the man next door.

You must try to do the same thing. If I were to tell you that you ramble, or that you always bore your friends by being a 'funny' man, you would be most cross about it, and you would consider me the world's worst teacher of public speaking. This is the way I shall try to help you solve your problem:

When reading the last chapter you may have discovered one of your own mannerisms about which you had hardly been aware. I want you to see now if you can type yourself. You are going to read descriptions of many kinds of speakers. They cover ninety per cent of all speakers. The other ten per cent are the men we want to hear. If you can hardly credit this, ask yourself this question: "*What percentage of speakers have I heard during the last year whom I really admire?*" I doubt if it's more than ten per cent.

I belong to a club well known for the quality of its guest speakers. We were chatting about speeches we had enjoyed, and an eminent author said that not one speaker in five was worth listening to. The others agreed with him. If that is the standard for regular speech makers, you will realise that there is much room for improvement. Without knowing anything about speech building or how to marshal your facts, you can become a better-than-average speaker just by learning to relax, and deciding not to be anything like the types of speaker I am now going to tell you about. Remember as you read about them, you must say: *Does it apply to me?*

The Rambler

He is the most common type of speaker. Like the rose of the same name, he branches off in all directions. A rambler once said to me, "I don't believe in prepared speeches. Just talk naturally, that's what I do, and I express the thoughts as they come to me."

That wouldn't be so bad if the thoughts were worth hearing. They rarely are from a rambler. The reason for this is that so few of us are good impromptu speakers. I don't believe that the rambler really is either. I believe that he does prepare his speech, and then 'overcome with the exuberance of his own verbosity' he tries to improve on his speech when he is already on his feet, and thus the ramble begins.

How to tell whether you are a rambler? A rambling speaker is always a rambling conversationalist. He will begin a story, and before he has finished it will bring in other subsidiary stories. For example, did you ever tell a story like this?

"Did you hear about Bob James—I mean his car accident? It was really terrible, you know. The car was completely smashed. Of course, I've known Bob for years—we used to spend our holidays together.

He plays a good game of golf too. He once nearly did a hole in one at Gleneagles. Of course, I don't know how it happened, because Bob is a first-class driver, but then you know what Bridges Corner is like—very dangerous. As a matter of fact I stayed nearby there for my honeymoon. Betty and I love the place and we often go back there. It's one of those quaint, quiet places—no trippers, no coaches. What was I saying? Oh yes, Bob's accident. He may lose his leg you know! He's in the local hospital. I remember I was in there when I had my appendix out. There was a very decent chap in the next bed to me, and he said . . ."

And so it goes on. Bob's accident leads to many, many other stories, one leading into another.

Now think about it. Do you ever tell a story that way? If so, you're a rambler.

It's easy to cure. Just stick to your story when conversing, and you will keep to your speech when you are making a speech.

The Monosyllabler

He speaks not so much in clipped sentences as clipped words. A word—a pause—a word—a pause, and so on. Possibly this kind of speech-making originated in the army, but to-day it hardly applies. Army leaders more often than not speak extremely well. No doubt, it was an effective way of giving orders at one time, or of modestly telling men that you would play ball with them if they played ball with you, but it is quite ineffective when used by a public speaker.

The Statue

He is in the minority, but no-one likes him. His attitude makes him appear aloof. He stands bolt upright as if encased in plaster. No movement for him, except an occasional nod of the head.

The cause? Usually, extreme nervousness. He gives no appearance of nervousness. It is all bottled up and, no doubt, his nerves are so taut that if he moved too much some of them might snap.

The statue is often looked upon, however, as a nerveless man, but even his aloofness, although sometimes attributed to the fact that he cannot suffer fools gladly, is basically caused by shyness.

If you are a statue, learn to relax. It will give you years of happiness.

The Asider

What an irritating man! We are sure that he is reserving his best quips for those on either side of him —or possibly, he is criticising us. When we laugh heartily he takes the opportunity to say something to the chairman, or to a friend. Throughout his speech he is continually half-turning away and saying something that we cannot hear. He has a quick mind, has the asider, and he knows how to use it. If you are one, do stop it. If you have anything witty to say, say it to us. If it is an unkind thrust, keep it to yourself.

The Too Pompous

He talks in platitudes and clichés. We could put up with that, but we don't like the way he makes us feel that he is doing us a great honour by speaking to us. Too many speakers—politicians especially—think they are doing us a favour by visiting us at our local halls. They are not! We are doing them a favour by making them feel important enough to be listened to. The pompous man is quickly typed. Every other sentence is, "I remember this," "I must remind you of that," "In all humility I must submit . . ."

That last hackneyed phrase is bad enough, but it is made worse because he conveys the impression that he is not one little bit humble, and would submit to no-one.

I know that you are not pompous. Why? Because I doubt whether a pompous man would ever feel the need to read this book. I have just put him in as a warning—that's all.

The Emotionalist

He is good. He holds our attention. He brings tears to our eyes. As his temper rages, we rage—for five minutes. Then we see through him.

A speaker should express his emotions. He should look sad when he expresses sad thoughts. He may thump the table when he feels strongly about his special subject—just once. It is when he goes on thumping tables and tear jerking for a long time that we begin to feel that he is not sincere. He may well be sincere, but we cannot credit it. We don't like continual appeals to the Almighty. We don't like waving arms all the time. We don't like to see ties ripped off, to denote that the speaker is working himself into a lather.

We don't mind a little emotion—in fact, we demand it. But it is when emotionalism gets mixed up with exhibitionism that we cry "Enough!"

The Blank

Now we go to the opposite extreme. Mr. Blank shows no emotion at all. His face is expressionless. We quickly begin to feel like a lot of little piggies in a sty, listening to Daddy Piggy laying down the law. We yearn for a smile, for an eye-twinkle, for a grin—for a sneer if you like. Anything, except that blank, uninteresting face.

This is hard, but at some time or another a Mr. Blank will read this book. Will he recognise himself? I hope so, for his sake.

LET'S THINK AWHILE

I am writing this in a bedroom in a hotel in Torquay. I am having a holiday. It is pouring with rain, but the view is perfect. I have paused in my writing to watch two fellow guests putting on the greenway down below. The pause has made me think. I have realised that I have been a little pompous, writing about faults in other speakers. I have read back and revised. Much of it I have retained however, because I do believe it does all of us good—all who have to speak in public, anyway—if we face up to facts. There are some more types to come. You can profit by the mistakes of others. I have done in the past. Let us, then, go on trying to see ourselves as others see us.

The Throat Clearer

I don't know which is worse, listening to him clear his throat or waiting for him to do it. Sometimes he makes it harder for us to bear by apologising after a 'clear'. Then the speech goes something like this:

Words—words—words—grr-grr—sorry—words—words—is it coming now? No, what has happened here then?—words—words—grr-grr—sorry . . .

The grr's may be caused by sinus trouble or catarrh —or too much smoking, or perhaps they have developed through nervous tension. It is tough to cure—I am a bit of a grr-er myself. But the effort to cure it must be made if we are to have a receptive audience.

The Funny Man

He is, possibly, the hardest man to cure, and we shall deal with him more fully in another chapter. He is determined to make us laugh. Story follows story— he is a walking joke-book. How many people do you know who can really tell a humorous story? One in ten would be an over-estimate, no doubt. That for speakers would be a wonderful percentage. It would be nearer one in fifty. You can check up on yourself easily.

Do you tell more than one story if you are in a group with others telling their pet tales? Do you hardly listen to the other fellow because you are racking your brain to think of a better one to tell?

If you do you risk being a *Funny Man* speaker. Take care. Once you start you will never stop, because you will think you are exceptional. You will be sure that you are the one and only truly *funny man*—they all think that!

The Starer

This is the speaker who fixes his gaze on one inoffensive member of the gathering and keeps staring at him during much of his speech. Alternatively, he stares at the ceiling and we all look up to see if, perhaps, an enormous crack has appeared.

Don't be a *starer*. They are frightening speakers.

The Whisperer

The only whispering speaker I have heard who achieved success was the lecturer in a showroom demonstrating hearing apparatus for a manufacturer of deaf-aid appliances.

"Speak up!" we want to shout out. Sometimes we do, and if the *whisperer* is a nervous speaker the result can be disastrous.

A speaker may have many faults and get away with them, but a *whisperer* must be a failure.

The Showman

Nothing nervous about *Mr. Showman*! He is tough and brash, and he is going to give us his act whether we like it or not. Off comes his coat, just to prove that he doesn't give a damn. If he feels like squatting on the floor with legs crossed, he'll squat. He will go down into the audience and will crack jokes with the chairman. He will do a jig, or stop everything while he calls for more wine with which to slake his thirst; or possibly he will drink two or three glasses of water running. He will throw things into the air and produce gadgets from his pockets. He is good—and he knows it.

A little showmanship certainly helps a speech along, but when it is overdone we look upon *Mr. Showman* as just a show-off.

The On-and-Off-er

You know him well. "Mr. Chairman, ladies and gentlemen, your policy and my policy are the right (glasses off) policies, and if we stand together (glasses on) we cannot fail (glasses off) to emulate our fore-fathers (glasses on) who set us an example (glasses off and twirling) of strength of character." (Oh dear, they're back on again!)

The *on-and-off-er* always has pages of notes which he cannot read without his glasses, while he obviously cannot speak when wearing them. He is a counterpart of the out-and-in-er. This speaker takes his hands out of his pockets and puts them back again. One well-known ex-Cabinet Minister did this fifteen times in a twenty-five-minute speech.

I wish I could tell you what he was taking out of his pocket. At first I thought it was a lucky charm, but later I had the feeling that it was a toothpick.

Don't copy these gentlemen—in fact, don't copy any of the speakers in this chapter.

CHAPTER V

Human Relations

Do you like criticism? Do you like being reprimanded? Do you like being made to look foolish? Do you like being told that your tailor is a poor craftsman? Do you appreciate being informed that you have no sense of humour? Do you really take kindly to the friend who tells you that you should take something for body odour?

Does it please you when someone tells you that you are good at something? Do you react favourably to a person who asks for your advice? Do you feel better when you receive honest appreciation?

These questions answer themselves. They touch the fringe of human relations. Many books have been written on this subject, and we have been teaching it for many years. How successful have we been? I shouldn't like to guess. If we can persuade one man in twenty to readjust his way of thinking and acting just a little, then we are satisfied.

There are two schools of thought on the subject. The first invariably repeats: *I am what I am and I can do nothing about it*. The opposite view to this, and the one to which we subscribe, is that each one of us has been given the right to alter his way of life, and to improve himself if he wishes. Those who feel that they cannot alter their mode of living are, apparently, in the minority, and in any event we cannot help them because they don't want to be helped. The majority of those who come to our Courses tell us that they do believe in the ability of man to improve himself, and they also believe in human relations—but they forget to add : In the other fellow.

For example, we have had many executives attending who agree with us that a measure of praise given to an employee brings excellent results. On several occasions I have been told by employees that it would be as hard to borrow one hundred pounds from their employers as to obtain one word of appreciation.

I remember one sales manager who made a speech on the value of courtesy. Not ten minutes later, during a coffee break, he was extremely rude to our telephone operator because she couldn't get a number quickly enough for him.

Some, of course, tell us that they feel it is hypocritical to smile when they don't feel like smiling. They may be right enough, but these men don't smile when there is no reason for them to feel glum.

The most difficult person to convince in this respect is the big business man. He has made his way in the world, and he wants everyone to realise that he's tough and speaks straight from the shoulder. Now here is a peculiar fact about this type of person : He prides himself on his bluntness and his direct manner of speech, but he can never accept any criticism of himself without losing his temper and fighting back. The day I meet just one of these straight-from-the-shoulder men who doesn't flush with annoyance when someone returns this straight-from-the-shoulder-stuff, perhaps I shall alter my opinion.

In spite of the difficulty that we all have in mastering ourselves sufficiently to carry out the principles of human relations, it is of such importance to the public speaker that he would do well to give it the utmost consideration. The majority of public speakers have to win over their audiences. There are, of course, exceptions. We all know men who have wielded tremendous influence from the platform, who have been bullies, liars and rogues. They are, however, few and far between. They usually have a cause for which they are fighting, and which lends itself to platform arrogance. They can attack others to give pleasure to their disciples.

This, however, is not for the average speaker. He must first win over his audience, so that they will be more responsive to the ideas he is going to outline in his speech.

Perhaps you don't think that that applies to you, because you are only reading this book to help you to speak reasonably well when asked to do so, at wedding receptions possibly, or garden fêtes, or at your masonic lodge. Do believe me when I tell you that years of experience in public speaking have made it plain to me that all speakers should understand something about human relations.

It is a question of doing a job efficiently or inefficiently. You don't want to give a wrong impression of yourself. It is a fundamental that we all like to be admired. Psychologists have been telling us that for years, and judging from the thousands of men and women from all walks of life who pass through our Courses, the psychologists are right. Most of them have told me that they don't give a rap for criticism, but they are always the first to beam with pleasure when they receive justifiable praise.

The man who tells us he is 'blunt' means, of course,

that he doesn't need flattery, but then only foolish people need, and can accept, flattery.

It is a deep subject, but the points given to you in this chapter are those which apply to all public speakers.

PUNCTUALITY

You would think that the importance of being punctual is so elementary that it is hardly worth mentioning. I wonder how many votes have been lost during election time by prospective Members of Parliament who could not keep to a time schedule.

Some little while ago I was helping in this direction, and I was surprised at the way the schedules were worked out.

Often, I heard these expressions:

"We can just make it if we cut question-time a little."

"Start the second meeting at nine. It's better for them to wait for me than for me to be kicking my heels."

Wrong thinking! Wrong planning!

When we are members of an audience we don't like kicking our heels waiting for a speaker to arrive. Neither do we want to receive a five-seconds-to-spare-breathless speaker. We want to feel that the speaker considers it an honour to address us. That he has given a great deal of thought to his speech, and that while we are getting into our seats, he has already arrived at the hall and is waiting to welcome us at the appointed time.

Those concerned with elections have told me that

this is not possible because of the pressure of time. I might have believed this had I not seen so much time wasted which could have been spent in travelling to other districts and getting ready for the next speech.

"I am always unpunctual," said a speaker with a smile. He thought it a good opening—an admission of a human weakness. It was nothing of the kind. It was merely an admission of bad manners.

Always be punctual. It is an act of courtesy which should be observed by all speakers.

SINCERITY

Everyone likes a sincere man. It is one of the highest forms of praise to be told that you are admired for your sincerity. Don't spoil it by flattery, or by working too strongly on the emotions of the audience.

Here is an example of how a good, honest speaker can make himself appear insincere. It happened at a conference. The hotel had been terrible. We had had an awful time. The town was depressing, and the weather abominable. In one of the final toasts, a speaker referred to the 'wonderful time we had been having' to the 'glories of the town' and to the fact that we should all be returning soon, if not for conferences, anyway for holidays.

If that speaker could have heard some of the remarks of the audience, he would quickly have realised that he had made a mistake.

He had obviously prepared his speech long before the conference, and the fact that it had been a flop had not registered sufficiently for him to make some last-minute alterations. That does not mean that he should have been unkind. He could easily have altered his speech so that, without hurting anyone, he could have avoided appearing insincere.

So many speakers spoil their speeches by insincere platitudes. Many speakers who make impromptu speeches (and this applies especially to those on the stage) invariably finish with *God bless you*, spoken with great fervour. It is said so often, yet we all know that it doesn't mean anything and that they don't care whether we are blessed or not. That kind of ending to a speech should be saved for the time when a person is speaking to his most intimate friends or relatives.

You may argue that it is difficult to be sincere at all times and not, at the same time, to be a John Blunt.

Look at it this way: John Blunt goes out of his way to tell people what he thinks of them. His opinions are often given without reason, and no-one has asked for his advice. The sincere man cannot see any sense in attacking or criticising others without reason. He reserves his criticism for the occasions when it is essential. He speaks sincerely about those things that he can be sincere about. On controversial points he keeps quiet, unless it is for the good of everyone that these points be aired.

The speaker at the conference about which I have just told you would have been just as wrong to have told the audience in front of our hosts that we were all upset at the dinginess of the town, and that we had not enjoyed ourselves. All he had to do was to confine himself to one or two aspects which had been enjoyed by everyone, and we should have been happy.

If you cannot feel sincere about your speech, you should not speak.

ENTHUSIASM

Jonathan Taylor had everything against him so far as public speaking was concerned. He was not fortunate enough to have had a good education. He had commenced work at fourteen. His appearance left quite a lot to be desired. He found it hard to smile—probably because of his early struggles. He had built up a good business in the building industry, and had decided to educate himself. He had always avoided making speeches, because he was so conscious of his faults. He came to our Course on Public Speaking.

You know what is coming next—it will, no doubt, remind you of the kind of advertisements which offer to change your whole life within forty-eight hours. That is what did happen to Taylor—although not quite so quickly.

He had one great asset, and that was his intense enthusiasm for everything he did. He didn't shine at the Course—in fact, he was below standard. But afterwards he did something that many others don't do—he practised relaxing. He did say, *Does it apply to me*, when he watched other speakers.

Taylor is not his real name. Recently I heard him give a talk, and he was first class. We did a little for him, but quite frankly, he made himself a success by his own great enthusiasm.

Arthur Stanley came to our Course with everything in his favour—public school, Oxford, good sporting record and a fine appearance. I don't think that we helped him a great deal. He had been sent to the Course by his father, the managing director of a public company. Stanley (again, that wasn't his real name) failed, because he didn't care much about speaking in public. He couldn't work up any enthusiasm for the subject, and we had to write him off as one of our failures.

All our lecturers are at one on this point. When a man has enthusiasm, he is half-way towards becoming a first-class public speaker. Every audience loves the enthusiast. They would rather listen to an ordinary speech put over with enthusiasm than to a first-class effort which is just one long drone.

Here, then, is another reason why a public speaker must take care when choosing the subject he is going to speak upon. If he doesn't really like it he will never sound enthusiastic over it.

TACT

Can you turn a tactless person into a tactful one? Possibly! However, I have never met a person who thought he was tactless. On occasion we all make mistakes in this direction. Tactless folk are quite often kindly people who would not willingly hurt anybody. They do it unintentionally. What, then, makes them tactless? Thoughtlessness, possibly! A lack of sensitiveness—yes, that is quite common. Wanting to be in the limelight? I have met some whose fault arose from wanting to be noticed. Lack of feeling? That is sometimes the cause.

Anyway, it is curable, provided a person is willing to think about himself for a while. We know that introspection is not always good for us, but how can we rectify our mistakes if we are unaware of them? Once more, you must ask yourself, *Does this apply to me?* Do remember that one tactless remark can turn a friendly audience into a hostile one.

The tactless speaker is invariably a tactless conversationalist. If you are tactless in conversation, you will be tactless on the platform. Ask yourself these questions:

When meeting Scotsmen have I ever referred to their reputed canniness either directly or by telling a story?

When meeting a Welshman have I ever quoted a Taffy jingle?

When meeting a person of the Jewish faith, have I ever said, "Some of my best friends are Jews," implying that I am one of the few who are tolerant towards them, although others aren't?

When meeting a citizen of the United States of America, do I make a weak joke about the fact that some of them may like to talk rather proudly of the wonders of their country?

These are the standard tests for a tactless person. People of this type usually give themselves away by referring to someone's country or religion soon after meeting them. If you mention the fact and try to correct them, they will answer, "Don't be foolish, they like jokes about themselves!" That is quite wrong. They may not mind jokes about themselves told by themselves, but they don't want to hear them from other people.

If you still don't believe me, show this passage in the book to a friend who comes, perhaps, from Scotland, or is a Roman Catholic, or is a coloured person, or is Jewish, and ask him to tell you honestly if I am right or not.

We have all been guilty of tactless remarks at some

time or another. What we must be sure of, however, is that we are aware that we have said something wrong. Then we can make up our minds never to do the same again.

Tall men don't like to be asked if it's cold up there.

Short men don't want to hear, "Why don't you get off your knees?"

If you can cure tactlessness in conversation, you will never be a tactless speaker.

TEMPER

How does this apply to a speaker? He may be dealing with a heckler or a questioner, and the interruptions may cause him to lose his temper. Whatever the reason, it is always unforgivable to do this as it means that the speaker has lost control of himself.

I have heard many speakers *apparently* lose their temper at injustice to others. They rage and storm, because they feel strongly about this. It is, however, usually an act, and they don't necessarily feel the rage within them at all.

Take the case of the questioner. The heckler we shall deal with in another chapter. Did you see a television programme some time ago during which a speaker lost his temper with a member of the audience who persisted with a question? It was commented upon by many critics next day. I was sorry that it happened, because I had had a high regard for that speaker until I saw him so unable to find words that he had to lose his temper. When this happens to a speaker, victory always goes to the member of the audience who has caused it.

Psychologists may tell us that it's good to emote in this manner now and again and to get things off our chest. If that is true, then do it privately, not in public.

CRITICISM

Hundreds and hundreds of times we have been asked for criticism.

"I can take it—tell me what's wrong."

"I want criticism—honest, constructive criticism."

"I appreciate that you don't like to criticise, but you have my permission to say what you think."

Sentences of this kind we hear regularly. But think about this: We have rarely given a criticism that has been asked for without the person concerned fighting back to prove us wrong.

Criticism from schoolmaster to scholar is easy. The same applies from employer to employee. In neither case can the person criticised answer back. But criticism between equals is always a problem. Sometimes a public speaker has to criticise members of the audience. He must take great care not to make the innocent feel guilty.

Every speaker might well remember these words of advice given to me many years ago:

Never criticise an audience if you can help it. If you must criticise, temper your criticism with praise.

PRAISE

We all like praise and honest appreciation. Few of us get enough of it. Flattery is accepted by only a few people, although many pretend to believe the flatterer.

When a speaker can honestly praise his audience he should do so. Perhaps for their communal spirit— possibly because the questions put forward plainly indicate the intelligent interest of the listeners; there are so many ways in which it can be done.

If an executive is addressing his staff and they deserve praise, then he should give it.

The easiest way to obtain a quick response from some audiences is to be vituperative about another person or body of people. It seems to help these audiences to get rid of their hate inhibitions. Politicians use the method regularly. It will give you more happiness in your years of speaking in public, however, if you adopt the other method, and help to win them over by honest appreciation of their efforts, or by praise of others.

BE HUMAN

Nobody likes an automaton. The listeners want a speaker to be a man of flesh and blood, with a heart, and with human feelings. That doesn't mean that they want him to have mannerisms or to act unnaturally. No, they want to identify themselves with him. They want to feel that he is liable to the same failings as they are. A little forgetfulness perhaps—a mistake over figures, to be quickly corrected by the audience.

It isn't insincere to make a mistake intentionally. It is often used by speakers to make sure the audience is following them. There is nothing that members of an audience like better than to be able to call out, "It was September, not October." "I'm sorry," says the speaker, "of course you're right." Or, "No, that was the Reverend Giles, not his father, Colonel Giles."

"How foolish of me," says the speaker, and then goes on with his speech.

Don't be too perfect. And don't be afraid to tell a story against yourself—one which will, perhaps, help you to teach the audience, by showing them that they need not make the same errors as you have made in the past.

AVOID THIS

Don't try to build up your own importance. No-one likes a man who boasts. But I am afraid that too many do make the mistake of talking about themselves to their own advantage. It is most commonly done by speakers who want some indirect reward from their speeches. Many speakers address conventions or associations and meetings with this thought in mind. Perhaps they are manufacturers of goods which would interest a proportion of the listeners, or they have ideas to sell.

These men invariably give the game away to the intelligent listener by the way in which they put in a plug, and boost themselves while so doing.

They would do themselves far more good if they never referred either to their business or to themselves. That would be appreciated, and might bring about better results than those achieved by self-advertisement.

The rule must be: Make the audience feel important, and play yourself down.

YOU—WE—I

An important rule for all speakers is one which applies equally to salesmen. A speaker is very much like a salesman. He is usually selling his ideas, whereas the salesman is selling his products. The rule is one we call

THE YOU-WE-I FORMULA

When talking on any subject, first think of the audience, and, therefore, use the word YOU as much as you can.

YOU will agree . . .

YOU achieve these results . . .

YOU know that . . .

If it isn't possible to use the word YOU, then use WE.

WE must try to do better . . . .

WE must examine all the points before arriving at a decision.

If WE can do the same every year . . .

Only when you cannot use YOU or WE, should you use I. Remember then,

YOU-WE-I

Human relations on the platform are most important, and are so often overlooked. We can never reach perfection, but you will agree with me that the right thing to do is to set a high standard, and get as near to that as we can.

CHAPTER · VI

Stand and Deliver

GEORGE said, "I can't breathe." Thereupon he took three deep breaths.

"What's the matter?" I asked.

"Nothing," he answered, "only I can't breathe."

"Never mind," I said. "It can't last long."

"And that," said George, "is all the sympathy I get from a man who spends his life teaching human relations."

"If," I said coldly, "you would stop for just one moment imitating a sergeant-major by inflating your chest and then looking like a hospital case when you prepare to let go, I might be prepared to sympathise."

"I hope it never happens to you," said George. "But perhaps it would do you good."

"Now do be normal for a moment," I went on, "and tell me what it is that you don't want to happen to me. And for goodness' sake stop breathing so hard!"

"I can't," shouted George. "That's the trouble. It began in the middle of my lecture. I suddenly became conscious of my breathing. I had to speak—gulp— speak—gulp . . . I must have sounded like a sword swallower rehearsing."

"That," I said smugly, "is because you don't breathe properly. Now let me show you how simply you can overcome your problem."

I proceeded to demonstrate to George how he should breathe correctly if he wanted to be a happy speaker. I knew all about it, because I had visited an elocutionist who had taught me how to breathe.

After completing the lesson for my brother, it was my turn to take a session. I walked upstairs feeling very proud of myself. The session began. It got under way, and I was enjoying myself—when it happened.

I began to be conscious of my breathing. I pretended not to notice, but I felt that I wanted to keep taking deep breaths. Naturally, I tried all the elocution lessons I could think of. I breathed from my stomach. I filled my lungs. I took deep breaths, and more deep breaths. I tried doing it normally. I wasn't enjoying myself at all.

All this happened many, many years ago. We were then training members of our own staff, and had not even thought of training others in public speaking. When our courses in public speaking did commence, we had long discussions as to whether we should teach students the right way to breathe in order to help them as public speakers. We decided against it, and we now feel that our decision was the right one.

We find that the problems of correct breathing are solved in a far better way by learning to relax. I do believe that breathing exercises help some speakers to develop better voices, but as against that, it makes others too conscious of something which should be quite natural.

No doubt it would be a good thing if the right way to breathe were taught at schools, so that voice production could be improved. When we are more mature in life, however, I do not think it helps quite so much and my advice is: Just go on breathing as you have done so far. You must have managed quite well.

The elocutionist will answer, "That's rubbish. Your public speakers must have good voices, and be able to speak clearly, and they can't do that unless they first learn to breathe correctly."

That's reasonable. But we don't teach elocution either. We did at one time, but we found that most people could not keep up with their exercises, and we also found that the vast majority of people don't need them.

You will gather from this that breathing exercises, mouth exercises, making coo-ing noises so that your voice will sound better, learning *How now brown cow* and repeating it several times a day doesn't come into our curriculum, and, therefore, you won't be reading much about it in this book. I agree that it is good to be able to speak like a radio announcer, but that is not our object. We want men and women to become good public speakers, and we have found from long experience that the majority of audiences don't care very much about articulation. They want to hear clearly, of course, but the fact that each word isn't spoken perfectly is of little importance to them.

This does not mean that a speaker should pay no attention whatsoever to his voice. We do advocate one or two principles which have helped many students to improve their delivery.

Remember that everything we teach has to stand up to one major test—*does it succeed*. Many companies send all their executives to us for speech training, but they always send one person to us first, to test out our ideas. These men have to speak in public, and if they don't make a success of it, we must take the blame. Long ago, therefore, we discarded theories which seem so good in print but which don't work out in practice.

The reason I am telling you all this is because I want to impress upon you that you need not go to extremes to become a good public speaker.

A GOOD DELIVERY

A good delivery is the art of presenting your speech in such a manner that the audience will not be bored, even if your subject matter is a little tedious. Any audience will quickly become bored if they cannot hear you properly. Some people have thin voices, some squeak a little, but most people speak well enough to be heard in an average-sized room. If the room is larger than average, then often a microphone is used. We don't like them very much, but we always advise anyone who feels that his voice is not too strong, to use them whenever he can.

It may look dramatic to have them switched off with an "I-don't-need-this-contraption" attitude, but that won't help if you can't be heard.

Tommy Armour, one of the great teachers of golf, advocates the use of a tee whenever possible. He says that it may make a player look professional and non-chalant when he throws his ball to the ground at a short hole where an iron can be used, but the fact is *all the top professionals tee the ball up whenever they can.*

The same applies to professional speakers. If they have the slightest doubts as to whether an audience will hear them, they will always use a microphone.

In an average-sized room you can be quite audible. Most people are inaudible because no-one has ever told them that they mumble and cannot be heard.

Check up

Do ask a friend if your voice can be heard reasonably well at a distance. Implore him to be honest with you. If he tells you that he can hear you, then you need not worry. If he tells you that you are inaudible, then this is what you must do about it:

RELAX

Yes, we're back to Chapter II. The relaxed man has a very resonant voice—far more than the man who is full of tension.

The man at the back

We have never found an easier way of training a quiet speaker—a mumbling speaker—a droning speaker—into becoming an audible speaker, than by the *man-at-the-back* technique.

This is not original. It has been taught for years. You will, of course, realise that we have not come to this conclusion without a great deal of trial and error. We have had special lectures on voice production, as I have already told you. There have been special exercises set for throat muscles and for relaxing throat muscles . . . But after a careful analysis we have found that simply by telling a speaker to talk to a member of the audience seated at the back of the hall, he obtains the best results.

Unless you are prepared to do a great deal of homework to improve your voice—and even these exercises may not bring about the result you desire—you won't find anything more simple than the method we advocate to make certain that you can be heard anywhere in the hall.

All you have to do is to make your speech to those in the back row. You can't keep this up all the time, obviously, but if you use it to begin with, and from then on direct your speech to the man at the back as often as you can, you won't have to worry whether you are heard or not. You won't have to shout to do this.

The reason why we cannot hear so many speakers is because they bend their heads and talk to those seated at the first few tables, or in the first few rows of the audience. When you hold your head high and direct your voice to the back of the room, you will be heard.

It's as simple as that!

Singing in the bath

Sounds silly? But singing in the bath makes you feel that your voice is quite resonant, and it can help you to strengthen those vocal chords.

Elocution

I have already written about lessons in elocution. No doubt it would be of assistance to some speakers to take them, but it can have a reverse effect.

At a meeting I attended demonstrations were being given by a team of people trained for the purpose. Two of the girls taking part had, obviously, had elocution lessons. Their articulation was so perfect that the whole act became rather laboured.

You may well answer that most actors and actresses study elocution and would fail without that study. That is probably true, but do remember that actors and actresses are more often than not bad public speakers. Without their scripts and their feed lines they are lost. When their script goes their voices are apt to lose confidence and we can hardly credit that they are the same people whom we have heard so clearly when they were playing a part. Another point is that their speeches are often spoiled because they are so obviously acting and not being natural.

If you have a really bad speaking voice, however, perhaps because of some circumstances in your youth, you may feel at a disadvantage when talking to others. In this case, elocution lessons will help you.

But do remember that a well-prepared and well-presented speech put over with enthusiasm will easily overcome audience reaction to a couple of dropped aitches.

ACCENTS

You have a Lancashire accent, or perhaps it is Yorkshire. Or is yours a Cornish burr? Possibly your intonation proves your Welsh ancestry. That's fine! Don't alter it. What's wrong with it, anyway? Shakespeare may sound a little strange to our ears if the actor has an accent, but so far as public speaking is concerned it doesn't matter at all.

A friend of mine living in the Midlands, knowing that he was going to be made president of his company's trade association, was determined to develop a southern university accent. The result was horrible! He was unnatural, and his audience was uncomfortable.

Accents can be delightful. If the purists were right, every American visitor would have to alter his voice, and every Englishman visiting America would do the same. What nonsense! Don't worry about your accent —be proud of it!

VARIATIONS

You must have been bored by the monotonous speaker. You don't want to be like him, do you? Then you have got to do something about it.

A speaker must vary the tone of his voice from time to time. It is tiring listening to someone talking in a flat, expressionless manner. You've got to do some homework to overcome that.

Reading aloud is the answer. It's a great pity that the days are past when father would read a part of a great classic each evening to the family gathering.

Start it up again if you can. If you can't, then read aloud to someone. I am sure your wife and children won't mind listening to you reading a good book to them. As you read, vary the tone of your voice to suit the passage you are reading. Also, read some passages faster than others.

A speaker should never keep to the same pace. At times you must speak slowly and deliberately. At other times you must step things up. Finally, you must put the right inflection on words. Give them life and warmth.

To understand my meaning, read the following sentences, and notice how your voice alters with each *No*:

"No, I don't want it."
"No, did she really say that?"
"No, I'm not as good as all that!"

"No! That's definite."

"No, I'd rather die!"

"No, I had to work late."

Is it clear now? Summed up then, a speaker must

(a) Vary the tone of his voice.

(b) Vary the pace of his speech.

(c) Use the right inflections.

SLANG

The answer as to whether you should use slang or not is simple—DON'T.

Professional speakers can sometimes bring in a slang phrase to drive home a point, but a newcomer to public speaking should cut out all slang words or expressions—cut them right out of your speech.

GRANDIOSE

Don't develop a florid style. Some speakers fall so much in love with long words and quotations that they become florid in their delivery. They want to be great orators, but audiences don't expect great oratory. What they do want is to listen to interesting speakers.

WORDS

Use simple words. If they are the right simple words they are far better than unwieldy ones of four or five syllables. Use easy instead of abstruse words, for example!

opposite instead of antithesis

gear instead of accoutrements

often instead of frequently
pay instead of remuneration
help instead of assist
raise instead of elevate
true instead of authentic
end instead of conclusion
sleepy instead of somnolent, etc., etc.

Obviously, you can't always use short words. There are times when a long word is the only one which will make your meaning clear.

Some people are afraid to use a long word which is the right one for the occasion, because of their fear of mispronouncing it. The way to overcome this fear is to use the word as often as you can before you have to make the speech.

The same applies to any word which you may find difficulty in pronouncing. Don't avoid it—use it.

YOUR VOCABULARY

Many speakers worry unnecessarily about their vocabulary and their grammar. With improved education facilities this fear, to a large extent, will gradually disappear.

One of our problems is to convince middle-aged business men that they need not worry about their lack of knowledge of the English language and its grammar. Many of these men left school at an early age and had to fight hard to achieve a measure of success. They are often made the butt for the witticisms of playwrights. Make them rich and make them common, this is the standard part for the father in any comedy or farce, or for that matter, in many a serious play as well. To a large extent playwrights are writing about a tiny majority who have achieved a degree of wealth which did not affect their way of life. The majority of people who have worked their way up are sensible, kindly, family men. What happens to them is that one day they find themselves called upon to make a speech. They begin to worry about their lack of education and they either decline the offer, worry themselves unduly—or else they try to put matters right.

When they try to put things right, because of their determination they nearly always succeed. Obviously, the audience want to hear a speaker who is not continually stuttering over words or mispronouncing them, but they will overlook quite a few of these shortcomings if the speech they hear is sincere.

This book is being written to take some of the worry out of public speaking, because most of that worry is unnecessary.

DON'T COPY

The occasion was a conference of the Incorporated Sales Managers Association. Members of the Sales Executive Club of America had been invited to talk about salesmanship, and sales managers and members of I.S.M.A. were also giving lectures.

One speaker from the U.S.A. was absolute dynamite. He was first class. One demonstration followed another. At one moment he had the audience rocking with laughter—the next listening seriously to his words of wisdom.

I began to feel sorry for the member of our Sales Managers Association who had to follow him. The expert from the States was a difficult man to follow. Many speakers would have tried to emulate him—tried to outdo him in showmanship. That would have been fatal.

The man who did speak next did nothing of the kind. He made a kindly and congratulatory remark about his predecessor and then gave his speech in his own matter-of-fact style. No appeal to the emotions—no dynamics—although I am sure he would have been quite capable of doing this.

The contrast was just right, and he was as successful as the previous speaker.

Never, never copy another speaker because he has a specialised method of delivery. If someone else makes a success of telling humorous stories there is no need for you to try to do the same.

One speaker may waltz about the platform and look effective, but don't copy him—you stay still, if normally you do stand still.

Be yourself, provided you have tried to perfect yourself, and then, if your delivery and presentation are good, you will have nothing to fear from other speakers.

A GOLDEN RULE

Write the following words on a piece of cardboard and stand the board up where you can see it every day before you make your speech:

I MUST REMEMBER TO BE HEARD BY ALL MEMBERS OF THE AUDIENCE, AND TO MAKE CERTAIN OF THIS I SHALL TALK TO THOSE AT THE BACK OF THE ROOM.

CHAPTER VII

The Price of Success

IT was about twenty-five years ago. The speaker was the managing director, and he was lecturing to his staff—I was one of the staff. This is what he said:

Anyone can be successful if he is prepared to pay a price for success. That doesn't mean that we can all become millionaires. It means that in our respective spheres we can achieve a measure of success. The shop assistant can become the shop manager; the salesman can become the district manager; the office manager can become the general manager; the shop owner can become the owner of a chain of shops. But always remember that the price you have to pay is a continual price. If you refuse to pay it you will not succeed, and then you will become jealous of the success of others. If you stop paying the price when you have achieved some success, then you will slip back. That is why some companies achieve success for years, and then profits begin to fall. It means that the driving force has gone, and the price is no longer being paid. Not more than one man in fifty will pay any price whatsoever to enable him to succeed. He is always demanding his rights, and forgetting his responsibilities . . .

He went on in this strain for some time. It didn't cut any ice with me. Several times I nudged my neighbour and whispered, "More pep talks. When is he going to stop?"

Now, when I look back upon this speech, I can only think that he was wrong in one respect—the odds he gave. One man in one hundred or more would have been nearer the mark.

You may feel now as I felt twenty-five years ago. If you are still striving for success the last thing you want to listen to is lectures on how to succeed. If you have achieved success you may feel that it is not within the province of a writer on public speaking to deal with this subject. This thought may well be in your mind: *Enough of this nonsense! Get on with the speech-building.*

You will find little trouble in mastering speech-building and the correct method of using notes if you try to master public speaking step by step, and you have much to do before you are ready to plan your speech. That is where the price of success comes in.

"But you said it was easy," you may argue.

Public speaking is easy, when tackled in the right way. But it can be made difficult if some of the preparatory work is short-circuited. I am afraid the fact is that if you want to be a successful speaker you must pay a price. Some of your leisure hours must be spent in doing homework.

Perhaps to some it would be better if i were to suggest that they call it their hobby. Part of what I have to write about may not apply to you, for reasons that you will see later, but if it does, then do your homework diligently. You cannot become a super speaker in six easy lessons. What I do promise you is that if you will carry out our teachings you will become a good, confident speaker in a very short time.

Before you even begin to think about writing a speech in full, carry out some or all of the directions given in this chapter.

Words

As mentioned in the previous chapter, you need not possess a very large vocabulary to become an efficient speaker. If, however, you want to enlarge your vocabulary, all that you have to do is to take a greater interest in words. Whenever you don't understand the true meaning of a word, look it up in the dictionary. Make a note of it in a notebook which you should keep for this purpose. Refer to the book now and again, and try to use the word on occasion. You can double your word-power in six months by doing just that.

Some teachers believe that you should seek out the derivation of a word. This can be of great interest to some people, but not to all, and once more I can only say that we have found the vast majority will not do this. Again, it is one of those things which we used to advise our students to do, but after a check-up we found that they did not continue with this type of research. The tiny majority who are so interested in the derivation of words that they will continue to do this, did it before they attended our Courses anyway. It would be easy to fill pages with word derivations, but if you cannot really become interested it would not help you. You will, however, find it simple and interesting to check words in a dictionary, and then to use them, and you will do that. Eighty-six per cent of our students told us that it becomes a standard and interesting part of their lives.

Incidentally, our research department keeps track of our students for many years, so that we can always base our arguments on facts.

MEMORY TRAINING

"I have a bad memory."

"I can't remember names, so how can I hope to memorise speeches?"

"Can you improve my memory?"

We hear these sentences over and over again at our Courses. We have heard them so often that I asked two eminent authorities, a medical psychiatrist and an industrial psychologist, if it were, perhaps, true that the memory of mankind is not as good to-day as it was one hundred years ago. They both felt that there was a basis of truth in this, and that the reason for the deterioration of our memory is because that part of our brain which we use for retaining memories, and bringing them to the conscious mind when we want to remember something, is not worked hard enough. They blamed newspapers, television, radio, the basis of modern living and a few other things. The psychiatrist told me that the case was more or less proved by the fact that it is so easy to improve our memory if we wish to do so. "Once a person begins to try to remember," he said, "and to interest himself in the things he wants to remember, and to practise remembering so that his brain is kept active in this respect, the memory immediately improves." And that works.

Make remembering a habit by spending a few minutes each day working that part of your grey matter which deals with memory.

At some time or other you must have played the following game:

Various articles are placed on a tray, and you are allowed to look at them for a minute or two. They are then covered up and you have to write down as many of the items as you can remember. The winner of the game is the one who remembers the most articles.

That is the way to train your memory. Play the game with yourself, if you like, for a minute or two every evening, and within a few weeks you will find a great improvement in your memory. It would, no doubt, have sounded much more professional to have written many pages on some special method of memory training, but we have found none better than this simple game. You can play it on journeys by merely looking around a carriage and then trying to remember the objects you have seen. You can do it with your friends at the office. You need not tell them about it—a quick glance at their clothes—think—check up. It's good fun and it's the easiest and best way of improving your memory.

A reasonable memory is useful to a speaker, but you won't have to memorise long speeches, so you need not worry about it. For all that, try to improve your memory, it will help you considerably.

Plan for yourself

You must think a lot about making speeches long before you are ready to make one. Once more, we have found no better method than to advise students to use yet another *minute* technique.

Before they worry themselves as to how a speech should be built up step by step, they will find it of great benefit to talk about any subject for a short while without giving any thought as to whether their presentation is right or wrong. It does not need to be a long speech—just *one minute*, but if you learn to speak fluently for one or two minutes on almost any subject, then speech-building will become easy for you.

Here are several ways of doing this:

Pick a word

Choose any word you like—for example, garlic, chocolate, grass, smiles, sea . . . Describe for one minute what that word conjures up in your mind.

Choose an article

When sitting at home in the evening, look round the room and choose any article you can see—a clock, a hat, a chair, a tablecloth—then speak about that article for one minute.

Fill in the gap

Choose two words—for example football and Eskimo. Now make a minute speech commencing with the word football and ending with Eskimo.

You might begin by saying that football originated in this country. You could then go on to express the view that other countries have profited by our teaching and improved our technique; and that might lead into the story you heard of an explorer who found football being played by the Eskimos.

Now see what you can do with the following sets of words:

Begin with *Tibet* and end with *handkerchief*.
Begin with *sand* and end with *tomatoes*.
Begin with *rabbits* and end with *Stonehenge*.
Begin with *cinema's* and end with *oak trees*.
Begin with *libraries* and end with *love*.

These simple exercises in speech-thinking will condition your mind for speech-making. It is of great help if you can find someone to whom you can make your one-or-two-minute speech. Don't do it in conversation. Stand up and speak for a minute. You may feel a little uncomfortable at this even in your own home, but do it in spite of the laughter of others. Do it until it becomes a habit. You will find these exercises will be of tremendous value to you. If you cannot find anybody to address, then you must make the speech to a mirror, but that is not nearly so good as talking to someone else. The secret is that you must stand up to talk.

ANALYSING A SUBJECT

Take any subject you like and see how many speeches you can make out of that one subject to different audiences. For example:

ADVERTISING

If you think about advertising you will find that a speech can be made on it in a variety of ways. Here are a few of them:

Who pays for advertising?
This speech could be for consumers, to show that advertising has often resulted in lowering of prices and more efficient production.

Press advertising or direct mail advertising
This could be prepared as an after-dinner speech to a body of sales executives. It could deal with the

claims of those who advise Press advertising against those who believe that direct mail advertising can bring better results under certain conditions.

Pictorial or long copy

You could make your talk on this subject to copy-writers and layout men. Do readers read long copy? Do they prefer a picture and a caption?

Advertising as a career

Obviously, this would be suitable for an address to young men about to start their business careers.

You will be able to think of many other aspects of advertising which can be used for speeches.

Now see what you can do with the following subjects:

> GARDENING
>
> GOLF
>
> MATHEMATICS
>
> ARCHITECTURE
>
> PRODUCTION
>
> FURNITURE

Work out how many speeches you could make on each subject and to whom you would address each of them. Having done that, make a minute speech on each of the headings you write down.

More one-minute speeches

You must keep on with this practice. It pays such handsome dividends. After all, if your hobby were painting and you did a little painting each evening, you would expect your family to appreciate your work.

Well then, get your friends to help you with your public speaking.

Once more I must appeal to executives. It is these men who need to speak well in public, and it is so hard to make them do these exercises. One or two each evening can help such a lot. Make a minute speech on the following subjects, dealt with in the previous chapters:

RELAXATION

MANNERISMS

DOES IT APPLY TO ME?

HUMAN RELATIONS

GO TO MEETINGS

Here is some advice which our students tell us is of great help to them in achieving confidence whilst learning relaxation: Remember, relaxation takes six months to master, but you want to speak before that time has elapsed. Go to as many meetings as you can, and during question-time, *ask questions*.

The act of standing up and speaking in front of a large audience will be a great help to you. It isn't hard to ask a question, and that, in a way, is the same as making a speech. In addition to this, join in every discussion you can. If you ask sensible questions and limit yourself to one question a meeting so that you are not looked upon as a limelight speaker, you will not lose any friends because of your obvious determination to speak whenever you can.

THE PRICE OF SUCCESS

Read the beginning of this chapter again. Whatever your position in life may be, you are still likely to profit

N.T.—

by paying the small price asked for in this chapter. One of our greatest sportsmen, whose life, he told me, was made almost unbearable because of the fact that he had to make so many speeches, wrote that these exercises coupled with relaxation had helped him to enjoy life off the field as much as on it. His wife bravely bore the brunt of listening to his two-minute speeches, and she joined her husband in telling me that it had all been well worth while.

CHAPTER VIII

Speech-Building Step by Step

THE village hall was crowded. Farm hands mingled with farm owners. Perhaps mingled is the wrong word. The farmers were in front, but the farm hands and their families resolutely refused to take seats in the first few rows in spite of cajoling on the part of Harold, the village constable, and William, the doctor's son, who had volunteered to see that we were all seated comfortably. We had come to listen to a political speaker who was going to tell us what he believed was the right policy for the land. Unfortunately, the Important Man himself had been taken ill at the last moment and had sent a retired brigadier to speak to us for him. We did not complain. All the speaker had to do was to give us the party policy on land, to suit both farmer and employees. Our pet heckler had turned up, so that we felt sure we were in for some fun. Our pet heckler was most impartial—he would heckle Labour, Conservative or Liberal without respect for party.

Brigadier X. arrived and we gave him a kindly welcome. He stood up and began by saying, "I'm afraid this speech will have to be impromptu. I have got some notes, but I can't read them." We all laughed dutifully as he cast aside a few crumpled sheets of paper.

Next he explained to us that he didn't know much about the land, except that we were all farming stock —the backbone of the country—and he could tell by looking around that we were happy and united. How was he to know that the A's never spoke to the B's, and that there was feudin' going on all over the village?

Soon he was recounting some exploits of his own in far-away countries. All very interesting, but it didn't give our heckler a chance. We were most disappointed.

This was a bad case of a speaker who had not taken the trouble to master his subject. Only one man in hundreds can give an impromptu speech, and he was not that man. Everyone knows that a speaker must understand his subject, or he should not speak at all. In this case it would have been far better if the meeting had been cancelled.

My advice to you is to refuse to speak about any subject which does not interest you, or which you are not prepared to master by study. When you are invited to speak, ask yourself this question:

WHY SHOULD THEY WANT TO LISTEN TO ME?

If you cannot find a good reason for the audience wanting to listen to you, don't speak. Be selective. Better to give six speeches a year which are good ones, than twelve, half of which are bad. Audiences will quickly forget your good efforts, but always remember the times when you have bored or irritated them. This often happens to people in the public eye. An author may become famous because of his books. Before long he will be asked to talk on subjects far removed from his writings. Too often he accepts these invitations in his search for popularity. It takes time for him to realise that an author need not necessarily understand the implications of subjects ranging from *Peace in our time* to *Does zoology help children?*

After-dinner speakers are just as bad. They are sometimes called upon to honour someone they hardly know. They talk on and on and on, when the audience is most anxious for the speeches to end.

This kind of thing loses friends instead of winning over new ones. The first essential for a speaker is to be familiar with his subject, or to have such an interest in it that he is prepared to devote a lot of time to research work, so that he can make a good speech.

You have been asked to speak. You like the subject, and you want to know now how to build up your speech. Here are the first three rules for you to remember:

1. Think about it for several days.
2. Research.
3. Ask questions.

Think about it for several days

It is a mistake to rely too much on research work. By simply thinking around a subject for several days, ideas will come to you which you will never find in a book. Let us take a simple example:

Although you have only lived in your district for a few years, you have won respect during that time, and have been invited to give the first speech at the opening of the cricket club's new pavilion.

First you have to think about it. What was the first match you saw? Did anything happen then which might be of interest to anyone? Can you call to mind some unexpected event which took place while the pavilion was being built? Who has played the largest part in the success of the venture? Can you tell about his drive and energy?

Don't think about what other people have told you at this stage. Just use your own knowledge of the club, the players, and how the pavilion was built. Keep your notebook handy, and jot down all the interesting points as you think of them.

Research

Can you dig up some little-known historical fact about the club? It isn't always a good thing to give past history, but on this occasion all the listeners will want to hear how the club achieved success. When was the old pavilion first built? How was it built? Did the members of the team put it up with their own hands?

Visit the offices of the local newspaper. Ask to be allowed to look through the back files. You may well be able to impart some information to the audience which may not be known even by the oldest inhabitant.

Ask questions

Audiences like to hear stories about themselves. They also like to hear their own names mentioned. Ask the vicar about the time he had to score fifty in twenty minutes to win a match. Ask the groundsman to tell you some stories about how the ground was developed. Try to find stories of determination which have resulted in the pavilion being built in spite of difficulties.

After this work has been completed you will have dozens of facts around which you can build your speech.

Now prune. Discard all those facts which you find you can do without—duplicate stories—historical facts which are of little interest to the audience; these must be abandoned to enhance the value of the one historical fact that is worth talking about. Remember now, you are planning your speech step by step, and if you keep to the steps you can't go wrong.

Here is another example of how to obtain the material for a speech:

You have been asked to make an appeal for donations for a home for aged people. The same formula applies—THINK ABOUT IT FOR SEVERAL DAYS.

What has happened to elderly people whom you have known—the well-off were, no doubt, able to look after themselves, but how about those old folk who were not well off? How and where did they live? Any stories there? Do you know of any old couples living with children, thus causing unhappiness for both families? That angle may be dealt with. Do you remember that poor old soul on television who said, "For years I have only lived for God and myself?" She was so much alone. Could that story be retold?

Research

Some statistics might help. Could any local authority or Government department supply figures to show the proportion of population who are over seventy now as against the proportion in, say, 1910? And what will the position be in twenty years' time? How does the State help? What part do hospitals play? How much does it cost to keep one inhabitant for one week? If you worked it on a monthly or yearly basis would you obtain more donations? Could you use the sentence: *Become responsible for one old person for one year*?

Ask questions

Ask the chairman of the home to give you some details about it. Ask the matron for stories about the inmates. Ask the inmates for stories about themselves. Ask the doctor to tell you about the fortitude shown by some of the inmates. Ask for names . . .

The formula, then, is quite simple and can be applied to any subject. Try your hand at roughing out the notes for the following speeches: Make up the details, it will help you to deal with any subject, so it is worth doing.

1. A speech before presenting trophies to winners at a boys' school.

2. A speech about your own work. (I once heard a fine speech by a factory worker who told us how he polished glass.)

3. A speech on photography to a camera club.

4. An after-dinner speech proposing the health of a specially-invited guest.

5. An after-dinner speech proposing a toast to the ladies.

6. A speech *What Parliament Has Done* (from the aspect of any of the parties).

So far, therefore, you have learned that a speech is an accumulation of facts, either thought out for yourself or found out from others. Having obtained this information, you have the framework of your speech.

Now the framework must be built upon. Before

doing that, however, you have to consider the type of speech you are going to make. Are you going to:

(*a*) impart information;
(*b*) persuade;
(*c*) inspire;
(*d*) make an after-dinner speech which might well incorporate all three, or perhaps just be something in a lighter vein?

The above, in the main, covers the majority of speeches.

Impart information

This comes very close to a lecture. However, many speakers do have to impart information so that listeners can form their own judgments. For example, a shop steward talking to the men in his union about the new rates is imparting information. A sales manager at a conference imparts information. A technician, talking about the technical aspects of his work, imparts information . . .

In a speech of this kind, some important points must be remembered.

(*a*) Don't try to cram years of experience into twenty minutes. Preferably, take one aspect of your subject and deal with that thoroughly.
(*b*) You must be ruthless, and cut and cut. We often elaborate merely to show how able we are. Keep to your time-table, and leave the audience *wanting more information*. Better that than that the speech should fail because the audience has heard everything and understood nothing.

(c) Don't talk over the heads of the audience to prove your ability. Only deal with intricate technicalities if the audience understands them.

I once heard a speaker talking in public on aerodynamics and not half a dozen people in the audience knew what he was talking about. He could have simplified matters considerably and cut out many words which only experts understand, or he could have refused to speak to an audience not made up of aerodynamic engineers.

(d) You must make every point clear. If you feel that you have not done so, you can repeat a part of your speech, but word it differently.

(e) However involved your subject may be, please don't be as dry as dust. Make your speech interesting. Anecdotes can be told to liven up the most difficult of subjects.

(f) You should summarise your main points both during the speech and at the end of the speech.

To persuade

When you have to persuade people to do something which they may not want to do, or who are not certain what action they should take, you have to remember that most of us react more to sincerity than to bludgeoning. You may be able to persuade by a purely factual appeal, but that is doubtful. These points should be remembered:

(a) Don't only appeal to reason. Remember that

most of us can also be persuaded via our emotions.

(b) When presenting facts, make sure that they are accurate.

(c) Build up your case as a barrister works out his brief. Think out every logical argument, and then try them out on someone before the speech.

(d) Prove something. Prove that, as A happened once, B is bound to happen now because you are asking them to take the same course as applied when A happened.

(e) All your reasoning must be based on benefits to the listeners if they are to be persuaded to take the line of action that you advocate.

(f) Bring out as much evidence as you can. For example, if you are talking about cruelty to animals caused by traps, give evidence by eminent authorities on the suffering that these things bring to animals.

(g) Give the opinions of others. If you are trying to persuade people to vote for prison reform, give the opinions of prison warders, psychiatrists, Members of Parliament, visiting authorities—anyone or any group of people who have expressed opinions favourable to your own case.

Inspire

This is the easiest kind of speech of all, because only when someone is really inspired by his subject will he attempt to inspire others. Do remember, however:

(a) The inspiration of a speech will last only as

long as the speech lasts, unless some points or facts are brought out which the audience can remember. If you want to inspire members of a community to work for Civil Defence, for example, your inspirational appeal to their loyalty, or your reference to those who fought and died for us, will hold the audience, but they may not take action subsequently. During the speech you must coldly tell them why, for their own good, they should do something about Civil Defence, and ally your inspirational talk to this.

(b) You cannot be inspired or give inspiration unless you feel strongly about a subject.

(c) Keep your speech short. None of us can be inspired for much longer than fifteen minutes.

After-dinner speeches

Most audiences listening to an after-dinner speech want to be entertained. Sometimes a serious subject is discussed, but this would come under one of the previous headings. When building an after-dinner speech, remember:

(a) Don't relate many funny stories one after another. One or two are quite sufficient.

(b) When you have finally prepared your speech, cut it in half. All after-dinner speakers speak much too long.

These are the only two points to bear in mind about after-dinner speeches. The speech, however, must be built up on the lines we suggest later in this chapter.

How far have we got, then, with our speech-building?

1. We must plan our speech by thinking, by research and by asking questions.
2. We must decide on the type of speech we are going to make, so that we shall know our aim.

SPEECH-BUILDING

You have your facts, and now you want to string them together so that you will be able to present an easy-flowing speech which holds attention from beginning to end. A speech is very much like a sale made by a salesman. The speaker sells the audience his ideas, and the salesman sells his goods. The good salesman keeps to a logical sequence when selling, and the good speaker does the same. The steps of the speech are:

THE OPENING
CREATION OF INTEREST
CREATION OF CONFIDENCE
THE BODY OF THE SPEECH
THE CLOSE

Each of these steps will be dealt with in separate chapters. Obviously, however, you must have a good opening to be followed immediately by some interesting point which will hold attention from the beginning. You don't want the audience to sit back and wait for something to happen.

Having to create confidence may sound strange to you. All speakers need not use the step, although the majority would be wise not to take everything for granted. It often surprises some well-known people

when they meet someone who has never heard of them
—but more about that later.

The body of the speech is not one step only. It may
be divided into several steps—six, for example. In fact,
you can divide it into as many steps as you have facts
to present and time available.

AN EXAMPLE

Assuming that you were asked to make a speech on
public speaking, you would set about your task in the
standard manner.

QUESTION. Why should they want to listen to me?
ANSWER. Because they want to learn how to become
    better public speakers.

Next comes the formula:

Think about it for several days

Is the story of Bill Johnson, now managing director
of A.B.C. Steel, worth repeating? He has said that he
owes a great deal of his success to his early studies of
public speaking. There was that occasion when the
van driver spoke so well about the relative values of
horse-driven vehicles and motor-cars. There was the
speech you heard by A, by B, by C—can you refer to
them? And so on.

Research

Quotations must be checked, facts obtained. Would
medical support be of assistance to prove that public
speaking helps to overcome shyness and nervousness?
What books have been written on the subject? How
many should be studied by a student? What is the best

way to build a speech? Check up on notable speeches of the past. Check up on mannerisms of other speakers. Check up on human relations of public speakers. And so on.

Ask questions

Will your listeners be novices? Have any of them spoken in public before? Are they interested in group discussions? How long has the society been formed? Why was it started? Are the members mostly working men and women? Who is the prime organiser? Have they already heard too much from previous speakers on speech-planning? Whom have they heard previously? What are they interested in?

Naturally, for the purposes of this example, I have only covered the ground very briefly. If *you* were going to make this speech on public speaking you would enumerate many more facts.

Next you must ask yourself a question. What kind of speech are you going to make? Are you going to impart information, persuade, inspire, or make an after-dinner speech?

Assuming that you are not going to speak after dinner, in other words, it won't be a light-hearted effort to entertain, then your speech will be one which will impart information. The society would not have invited you unless the members had been keen on public speaking. It is for this reason that you will not have to worry a great deal about the inspirational value of your speech.

Having decided to impart information, you now have to make up your mind what facts to leave out. Should the Bill Johnson story go in, or in view of the fact that a great deal of inspirational value is not needed, is it best left out? The story of the vanman and his sincere manner of speaking—should that be left out?

The answers to the questions you asked of several members of the society about previous speakers have informed you that many of them have dealt with speech preparation and word power. You decide to cut out these items and to talk about human relations.

Now you are ready to break down the speech into steps. The following might well be your brief notes:

Opening. The YOU appeal, i.e. you will talk directly to the audience about themselves.

Interest. The Bill Johnson story. You are bringing this in now for interest value, not for inspirational value.

Confidence. Brief mention of tour of the U.S.A.

Main body of speech.

    A. Mannerisms.

    B. Appearance of speaker.

    C. How to win over audiences.

Close. Tribute to the work done by William Smith, who is the main organiser of the society.

Progress is being made. You have a mass of notes. You have discarded much that you did not wish to use, and you are left with the seven steps. You are going to speak for thirty minutes.

A SENTENCE

You will find that the best policy is to write out a good opening sentence for each fact, and only when

you are satisfied with your main sentences should you
go ahead with the building of your speech.

For example:

Opening. Thank you for looking so enthusiastic. That is
of great help to a fellow speaker.

Interest. Some of us learn public speaking as a hobby.
Others know that it will help us in our business.
Bill Johnson told me . . .

Confidence. Recently I was in New York lecturing to . . .

Human Relations. We all like a speaker who, we feel,
likes us . . .

Mannerisms. Have you ever watched a fidget at
work? . . .

Appearance. A speaker's appearance is his shop window . . .

How to win over the Audience. Give praise when praise is
due. Charles Schwab said . . .

Close. Mr. Smith did me a good turn when he asked
me to speak to you, and this is why . . .

Now you have your framework, and you can work
upon it. But just to give an opening sentence isn't
enough. Each statement you make must be proved,
and must be driven home. You must, therefore, build
around each fact or sentence, and you do it in this way:

    (*a*) You give statistics to prove your point.
    (*b*) You present evidence to prove your point
    (*c*) You give an historical fact.
    (*d*) You use an anecdote.
    (*e*) You tell a humorous story.
    (*f*) You give an analogy.
    (*g*) You give a quotation.
    (*h*) You recite a poem or part of a poem.

There is no set order, and obviously you will not use all the speech-builders. Possibly you will use only one —you may use statistics for example, or you may use two points such as statistics and an analogy. You may even use three—a humorous story, a quotation and statistics. But you will rarely use more than that.

Let us think again about your speech on public speaking and see how this formula works out.

You may be talking about the need for a good memory on the part of public speakers.

Sentence. You must do your best to improve your memory.

Anecdote. After all, cloakroom attendants have to have good memories and what they can do, we can do. I asked the attendant at the Golden Dome Restaurant the other day, when he gave me my hat, how he could remember that the hat was mine, as he had not given me a ticket. He answered very briefly, "Because *you* brought it in."

Analogy. A public speaker, after all, who has a bad memory can be likened to a mariner without a compass. He may start off by knowing where he is going, but he loses himself half-way.

Quotation. Dorothy Parker said, *Women and elephants never forget.* We should try to make her add, when next she revises *Ballade of Unfortunate Mammals* 'and also public speakers'.

Here are some more examples:

ROAD SAFETY

Sentence. We all think that we are safe drivers.

Anecdote. Not long ago I stopped by a crowd. They

were looking at a child—she was dead. The driver
of the car was standing by. He, too, no doubt,
thought that he was a safe driver.

Statistics. Eighty-two people were killed or injured in
the area of this county last year. They were all
killed or injured by 'safe' drivers.

PRISON REFORM

Sentence. It is simply a question of believing either in
fair punishment or revenge.

Poem. Wilde wrote:

> I know not whether laws be right,
> Or whether laws be wrong;
> All that we know who be in jail,
> Is that the wall is strong;
> And that each day is like a year,
> A year whose days are long.

Yes, being kept away from one's fellow men is, in
itself, a terrible punishment.

WELCOME GIVEN BY THE PRESIDENT OF AN ASSOCIATION

Sentence. Welcome to all four hundred and six of you.

History. Just thirty-eight years ago Mr. Brown, who is
sitting opposite me now, welcomed the first six
members of our association . . .

You will realise now that speech-building is not
difficult and can be most enjoyable, if you keep to the
formula given in this chapter.

But you want to do something more than just not

make a bad speech. You want to make a good one. Many speakers use the right ideas, but spoil their speeches by giving boring statistics, or telling stories of little interest to anyone. It is *how* you use your anecdotes, statistics, and analogies, which can make all the difference between a good or an ordinary speech.

This is the way to use them:

Statistics

Statistics can be as dry as dust, or they can be live and interesting. Talk round figures. It may sound very knowledgeable to say one million nine hundred thousand nine hundred and eighty-four and three-quarter yards of material were used in the new shop, but it's far better to get on with the speech and give the figure as nearly two million yards. The only time you need quote exact figures is if it is vitally essential that the audience have the exact figures, and that is very rarely.

If your speech is being reported and you want to be quoted as giving exact figures then, of course, you must be precise. But you must make your figures interesting. For example, you might say, "A thousand new customers were added to our list last year." Don't you think it would sound very much more effective if you said, "Last year a thousand people began to realise the wonderful qualities of our shoes—a thousand extra customers walking the way we want them to walk—comfortably. In fact, a walking advertisement for our business . . ."

This turns the customers from units or numbers into human beings. When giving figures, try to compare them with something. People often find it difficult to grasp the meaning of a million of this or five million of that. Even the implication of a hundred thousand might be hard to assimilate. Give the audience a comparison that they can understand.

You may speak of thousands being killed in an earthquake and your statistics would have little effect on the audience. But if you were to say, "Think of this district. North we have Blixton, twenty miles south is Hart, fifteen miles east we have Wells and twenty-six miles west is Trent. Imagine walking or motoring over the whole of that area and finding no-one living— not an animal, not a human being. That's what my figures mean."

When you congratulate Harry Hoggs on his wonderful bowling achievement at the end of a season, the number of balls bowled may mean a lot to the cricketers present, but there may well be many people listening who are not cricketers. His sterling work, carried on week after week, might be more appreciated if you said, "Harry takes a long run to the wicket. I've measured it exactly. We all know the number of overs he has bowled this season—he hasn't spared himself for the club. Do you know it is the equivalent to his running to Manchester and back. Some man, our Harry!"

Yes, you can make statistics live.

Quotation

A good and apt quotation will help you to bear out one of the main facts you have given—but it must apply to the fact. Some speakers have favourite quotations which they use and which have little bearing on their arguments. Don't do this. Also, do check your quotations. There is no sense in misquoting when a few minutes' check with the *Oxford Dictionary of Quotations*, or a similar work, will put matters right.

Don't use hackneyed quotations. When I was in New York I heard three speakers quote Patrick Henry —*I know not what course others may take; but as for me, give me liberty or give me death*. Working on this average, that quotation must be used by many, many speakers. It is a truly wonderful statement, but if used again and again by people speaking on a variety of subjects, the quotation loses its effect.

At one time many speakers were borrowing Sir Winston Churchill's famous tribute to our Air Force: *Never in the field of human conflict was so much owed by so many to so few*.

It doesn't enhance the value of a speech when such a quotation is used to emphasise, perhaps, a triviality.

Anecdotes

When relating an anecdote, try to make it live. You can best do this by bringing yourself into the story, whether it is humorous or otherwise. If you make it sound real, although the audience know that it is only a yarn, it will have much more appeal for them.

The anecdote can be built up by referring to:

> Someone you spoke to.
> Something that happened to you.
> Something you saw.

Here is a story which might well be read in any magazine:

Shopper: How much are the lupins?
Florist: Six shillings a dozen.

Shopper: Did you raise them yourself?

Florist: Yes, madam, they were four-and-six a dozen
    this morning.

Not very humorous, but this is how it was used by
a speaker at a local flower show:

"I walked into old Tim's shop this morning and
asked him the price of his daffodils. Old Tim—I can
see him winking at me now—pointed proudly to a
bowl and said, 'They're six shillings a dozen.'

'They look fine, Tim,' I said, 'did you raise them
yourself?'

'Sure I did,' he answered. 'Sure I did! They were
only four-and-six this morning.'"

Still not very funny possibly, but it does show what
can be done with a very ordinary story.

Here is another example:

The speaker was speaking to a crowd of sportsmen,
and he well knew that they liked nothing better than
to hear of his shortcomings. This is how you might
have read the story he told:

An Englishman was shooting in the Highlands. He
was not doing at all well. MacTavish, the gillie, became most disgusted. Finally, the sportsman shot
and a bird fluttered to the ground. He looked trium-
phant. "I killed that one all right, anyway," he said
proudly.

"Serves it right," said MacTavish, "for getting in
the way of your shot."

This is how the speaker told the story:

"When I was younger I used to boast quite a bit,
as some of you may well know, but I lost all that after
a shoot to which I was invited. I went up to Scotland
full of enthusiasm and told everyone that I would have

a record bag. Because of my bragging I was given one of the best gillies, MacTavish.

He was a man of few words and these became fewer as I missed time and time again. I blamed everything from my new gun to the fact that I was wearing the wrong glasses. At long last one solitary bird fluttered to the ground. I felt much better. 'I killed that one all right, anyway!' I said as I turned to MacTavish with face aglow.

He spoke for the first time in twenty minutes, with a grunt. 'Serves it right,' he said, 'for getting in the way of your shot.'"

Don't you agree that told that way the story sounds much better?

This method does not only apply to humorous stories. It can be used for any anecdote, from relating what happened to your little nephew when he dashed across the road, to the canning of meat in Chicago's largest cannery. The eye-witness story always appeals.

Remember then, refer in your anecdote to yourself in this way, or to someone you have met, to something that happened to you, or to something you saw.

WRITE IT OUT

You have now built up your speech, step by step. Go through it once more. Make certain that you are satisfied with it. Then write it out in full from your notes. Having done that, don't read it again yourself, but get someone else to read it to you. Still you must not be satisfied, although perhaps two or three weeks have passed since you were first invited to speak.

Now you will have to polish it up. The best way for

me to help you to do this is to take each step and deal with it separately. That I will do before dealing with the question of whether it is advisable to memorise your speech or to work from notes.

Here are the main points for you to remember in speech-building:

1. Know your subject.
2. Ask yourself the question: Why should the audience want to listen to me?
3. Before preparing a speech:
    (a) Think about it for several days.
    (b) Research.
    (c) Ask questions.
4. What kind of a speech are you going to make?
    (a) Impart information.
    (b) Persuade.
    (c) Inspire.
    (d) An after-dinner speech.
5. The main steps must be:
    The opening.
    Creation of interest.
    Creation of confidence.
    The body of the speech (which will be sub-divided into several steps).
    The close.
6. Write down the main facts which will apply to each step.
7. Cut out facts of little importance.
8. Devise a good opening sentence for each fact.
9. Elaborate each sentence in this manner:
    (a) Give statistics to prove your point.
    (b) Present evidence to prove your point.

(*c*) Give an historical fact.

(*d*) Tell an anecdote.

(*e*) Tell a humorous story.

(*f*) Give an analogy.

(*g*) Give a quotation.

(*h*) Recite a poem or part of a poem.

You need not use more than one, two or three of these and you can place them in any order.

10. Remember these rules:

Statistics—make them live.

Quotations—make them apt.

Anecdotes—bring yourself into the story.

Read this chapter again. Now I want you to build up a speech before reading the next chapters. What shall it be about?

Well, you can make one up on any subject which interests you or, alternatively, use the following:

A speech to be delivered to a group of students on

THE WELFARE STATE

I shall refer in later chapters to this particular speech, although you may have written one on another subject.

Are you getting ready to turn over to the next page? Well don't! Write your speech first.

CHAPTER IX

The Opening

HAVE you ever had to ask your bank manager for an overdraft? A bank manager, who attended our public-speaking course, told us of one conclusion at which he had arrived after seeing many of his customers who visited him on such a mission. It was that they had all prepared an opening sentence.

This is the way he put it: "Some ramble, others produce evidence of the need, a percentage tell a cock-and-bull story, a few tell us about their securities, but they all have this point in common: Every one of them has obviously thought out what he considers to be a dramatic, spectacular, or effective opening, which immediately follows the usual pleasantries."

This, of course, not only applies to people seeking overdrafts, who, no doubt, do think for days in advance of what they are going to say, it also applies to many other things that we have to do. The young man about to propose will think about his opening sentence for days and weeks. He will alter it time and time again. If we want to reprimand someone, we think for a long time about what we shall commence by saying.

It seems, therefore, that most of us do pay great attention to the first few sentences we have to speak on any special occasion. People do this who never marshal their facts for the subsequent discussion. The reason is that many people think that a good opening means everything, whatever the discussion may be about. As one man said, "It gets me started, and that's all I need."

Unfortunately, many public speakers, while fully aware of the importance of a good opening to their speeches, believe that any standard opening is good enough.

What kind of opening sentence did you use when you (I hope) worked out your speech after reading the last chapter? This chapter is designed to help you to polish it up and to improve the opening sentence of every speech you may make in the future.

Don't bring everything in

The principal speaker stands up. "Mr. Chairman," he begins, "Lady Bloggs, Sir John Bloggs, Mrs. Phipps, Mr. Blenkinsop, Mrs. Blenkinsop, Mrs. Blenkinsop's children, ladies and gentlemen . . ."

This, of course, is an exaggeration, but we have all heard something approaching it. Too many speakers bring in too many names when they begin their speeches. This isn't necessary. The fewer the names you introduce at the beginning the better.

Mr. Chairman, ladies and gentlemen is sometimes quite sufficient, although on many occasions you will have to introduce one other name only, following the words '*Mr. Chairman*'.

Apologies

Those apologies! You hear them over and over again. Make a firm rule, *never* to apologise about your speech. Here are a few examples of what we have all heard:

"Unaccustomed as I am to speaking in public . . ."

"I'm not much good at this kind of thing . . ."
"I won't keep you long." (They usually do not keep their promise.)
"I'm more used to action than words . . ."
"They dragged me into this . . ."
"I don't know why they asked me to speak . . ."
Never apologise.

Start on a low note

It is often a good thing to start a speech on a low note. Many a speaker has begun in a dramatic manner, and then fizzled out.

A number of good speakers lower their voices a little to begin with, although they only do this if they are confident that they can be heard in all parts of the hall. Lowering the voice does not mean mumbling. In point of fact, the lower tone can be heard just as distinctly as a high-pitched voice. By starting on a low note the speaker gives the impression that he has devoted careful thought to his subject, and he is going to treat it with the deliberation it deserves.

This is not a standard rule, but it is one to bear in mind for the more serious kind of speech.

HOW TO BEGIN

When reading the following openings do remember that the kind you use will depend entirely on the type of speech you are making and on your own personality.

The Informal Opening

This is always effective. To give you an example:
The speaker may be sitting next to Major Wiggs. As

he stands up—something he takes his time over—he smiles at his neighbour and begins:

> "Mr. Chairman, ladies and gentlemen, I was just saying to Major Wiggs that it is obvious that you are all deeply interested . . ."

The speaker is in his stride right away. It all seems so informal that no-one realises that the speaker has probably specifically commenced the conversation with his neighbour for this purpose. It is bound to bring a nod of agreement from the Major, who acts quite naturally because he is not aware that he is taking part in an *informal opening* to a speech.

The Question Opening

This is designed to make the audience think. People become alert when they start to think. Even the sleepiest member of the audience sits up when asked a question.

A speaker was asked to address the sales force of an insurance company. He took a risk with his opening as it touched upon a delicate subject, but this is how he began with a question opening:

> "How much income tax did you pay last year? Will you please think about it for a moment. You shouldn't have much difficulty in remembering how much was deducted from your income."

There the speaker paused. Then,

> "Right! Can you remember the amount? Well not one of you is paying enough, and I am acting as an unpaid member of the Inland Revenue Department. I want to see that they get some more

from you, and to do that I must help you to increase your incomes."

Here are some more *question openings*:
The following, used by a speaker talking about the National Playing Fields Association:

"Have you ever tried playing football in plimsolls on rubble?"

A speaker on astronomy began in this way:

"Have you ever looked upwards on a starlit night and said, 'I wonder what it's all about?' Just think for a moment. Have you done that?"

Now work out some *question openings* for yourself. Plan them on the assumption that you are going to make speeches on the following subjects:

Boxing is a dangerous sport.
The export drive.
A charitable appeal.
How I prepare my speeches.

The Mind-Reading Opening

This is sometimes used by speakers who know that they are facing a highly sceptical audience. Here is an example:

"Gentlemen, if I were sitting where you are sitting, without possessing knowledge of the facts which I possess, I should feel just as antagonistic towards the speaker as you may well do. I appreciate the way you may be thinking, but I know that you will give me a fair hearing . . ."

If ever you feel that an audience has a preconceived idea which may detract from their listening intently to you from the beginning of the speech, then the *mind-reading opening* can be quite useful.

The Humorous Story Opening

Be careful. Remember what I wrote about the *funny man*. The *humorous story opening* is excellent, if you can tell a story well and you have a good story to tell. If it falls flat, however, and doesn't get a good laugh for you, it can upset the balance of your whole speech.

If, on the other hand, you can get the audience laughing right away, then you have won a quick victory. Do remember that your story MUST tie in with the speech. It must lead into the main sentence quite smoothly.

The Local Colour Opening

Many people think the *local colour opening* has been overdone and, indeed, it has been by many speakers who have spoiled it by their flattering remarks. It is for that reason that you need to take care when using it.

This is how it was used by Stanley Baldwin:

> "However hardened a speaker may be, and however many places he may have spoken in, he cannot rise for the first time in Birmingham Town Hall before a Birmingham audience without a thrill of emotion. For a generation this great hall was associated throughout England with the names of two of our greatest orators, John Bright and Joseph Chamberlain!"

There is no flattery there. Humility, yes, because he

went on to say that, although he would fall short of their eloquence, all speakers must be stimulated by their example.

By talking about their own hall at the very beginning of his speech in such glowing terms, he made his audience feel very proud.

Historical Openings

Some examples right away:

> "When the Club began over twenty years ago . . ."
> "We have had many ups and downs in this Association . . ."
> "When first we began our monthly luncheons we all thought . . ."
> "It was first pioneered by X, thirty-six years ago, when he discovered . . ."

Do you get the idea?

An *historical opening* only means that the speaker relates some past facts, then brings the audience up to date, and gets on with the main point of his speech. If it is kept brief it can, by reviving some old memories or by painting a picture of what has gone before, get the speech off to a good start.

It is, however, also used by bores, who send everyone to sleep. They delve so deeply into the past—history which we all know well—and they go on for so long, that we begin to wonder if they will ever reach the body of their speech.

Keep the *historical opening* snappy, and it is very useful.

The Factual Opening

Used by many speakers, this opening takes you into your speech right away.

Here are some examples:

> *A Speech to a Society for the Preservation of Bird Life*
> "Oil is a killer and a very painful death it brings. It is estimated that twenty-six thousand birds at least died in agony along this part of the coast last year because of it, and we know that this can be avoided . . ."
>
> *To Engineers on the Care of Machinery*
> "A micron is only a thousandth part of a millimetre in size, but enough dust particles of that dimension can ruin the most expensive machine in a very short while . . ."
>
> *At a Variety Artists' Benevolent Fund Meeting*
> "Seven shows a day for two pounds a week—that's what many an old-timer thought was living in luxury . . ."

Now you see if you can compose some *factual openings* for speeches on:

> How to make a garden pay.
> The value of international sport.
> How to help older people to remain in industry.
> Slum clearance.

The Quotation Opening

An apt quotation can get you off to a good start. All that you are doing when using this opening is reversing our speech-building formula. You are giving your quotation first and you will then have to give your main sentence explaining your reason for giving the quotation.

The following are some actual examples:

On Bureaucracy

"*When law ends then tyranny begins,* said William Pitt. We have our law, but we have our tyrants as well. Pitt could make no allowances for them because bureaucracy is something which has really come into its own during the last ten years."

On Leadership

"*His heart was as great as the world, but there was no room in it to hold the memory of a wrong.* Emerson wrote that about Abraham Lincoln. What a lesson for some of the world leaders of to-day!"

On Education

"Will Rogers once said, *There is nothing so stupid as an educated man if you get off the thing he was educated in.* But we know that to understand one subject thoroughly, one must make a careful study of many. We don't want one-subject children . . ."

This type of introduction is easy and effective. Easy, because it doesn't take long to find a suitable quotation, and effective, because it is surprising how many people believe that a speaker is so knowledgeable that he knows a number of quotations by heart.

See what you can do with the following speeches: All you have to do is to find the apt quotation first.

> Juvenile Delinquency.
> Philosophy.
> The opening of a bazaar

The Stunt Opening

I once saw a speaker stand up, blow a trumpet to the amazement of the audience, and then begin by saying:

> "Now I've blown my own trumpet, so I'm going to talk about you . . ."

Strange to say it was quite effective, but my advice to you is: Don't use *stunt openings*.

The Topical Opening

This is similar to the informal opening. The speaker begins by talking about something which has happened shortly before. For example:

> *On Building New Roads*
>
> "So Arsenal won after all. That is of great importance to many people, but I wonder if those people ever think about the importance of building new roads. The time will come when they won't be able to get to their football matches unless something is done about this . . ."

Here is another:

> *On Rebuilding a Parish Church*
>
> "I hope your homes are not flooded—mine is. I have just heard that we have been through the biggest cloudburst for a hundred and sixty years. That's a long time. Almost as long as we have been trying to solve the problem of rebuilding the parish church . . ."

Shock Openings

This is a good way of beginning if the speaker is faced with an apathetic audience. It is sometimes even useful for the after-dinner speaker, when the diners have dined too well. Because it begins by a statement completely opposite to what the audience expects to hear, they usually sit up and want to hear more.

Some good examples of actual *shock openings* are:

At a Cycle Club Meeting
"The bicycle is a menace to every road user and a law should be passed to prevent its use . . . I mean, of course, when in the hands of those who have not yet been taught road-traffic rules . . ."

At a Parents' Meeting at School
"Education is useless, and a waste of money—unless it is backed by the right kind of teaching at home . . ."

On Exhibition Advertising
"Exhibitions are the most expensive form of advertising. Why? Because so few executives take the trouble to see that everything connected with their stand is as it should be, and that the personnel are properly trained . . ."

Now you find some *shock openings* for the following speeches:

A trade dinner—any kind.
A speech to authors by an important critic.
Industrial research.

Arouse Curiosity
Most of us are curious by nature. Arouse our curiosity and we are interested. Like many other openings, it covers two steps. It is an introduction and it arouses interest.

For example:

Addressing a Local Chamber of Commerce

"Over every shop in this neighbourhood there is an invisible sign. What is written on it? See if you can think that out. You are not sure? Well, it says: *I am here to make money, and everyone who can help me to do that is heartily welcome.* But do you make your customers as welcome as you should do?"

The 'YOU' Opening

One of the best openings of all—the YOU-WE-I formula is used right from the beginning.

To Builders

"You are builders. That is something to be proud of. Why? Well, if we walk right out of this building we shall see a new block of flats which some of you have helped to erect . . ."

On Design

"You have come here because you are interested in design. If I were to visit your homes I am quite sure that I should find pictures just right for the room, curtains which blend perfectly—yes, and furniture which shows good taste and good buying. How do I know this? You wouldn't be here unless the design of all things was of interest to you . . ."

You can't go wrong with the '*You*' opening.

The Story Opening

We all like a good story—not necessarily a humorous story, but something interesting. And most of us have a story to tell of something which has happened to us.

This is how a speaker began a talk on the safety of pets:

> "When I was motoring to Exeter I ran into a thick mist. It was impossible to see more than a couple of yards ahead, but I had to be in Exeter by ten o'clock. Suddenly, out of the mist there loomed up at me . . ."

Would you like to know what loomed up out of the mist? Well, so did the audience.

Of course, with this kind of opening the story must be linked up with the speech.

WHAT OPENING TO USE

You have been given various openings used by different speakers. Which one to use? Obviously, as I told you at the beginning of the chapter, this must depend on your speech and on your temperament.

Try not to keep to just one kind of opening. Give yourself greater experience by introducing your speeches in various ways on different occasions.

Besides the openings described, there are other standard openings. The *Thank You Opening* is used by speakers who wish to thank a previous speaker for his remark about them, or a committee for asking him to speak. Keep this opening short.

Some speakers produce exhibits which help them to begin. Others pay compliments . . . Executives sometimes commence by complimenting their staff on the work they have done.

It doesn't matter what opening you use, if it suits

you, if it links up with the speech, and PROVIDED IT DOESN'T TAKE UP TOO MUCH TIME.

> NOW REFER TO YOUR SPEECH ON THE
> WELFARE STATE AND POLISH UP THE
> OPENING.

CHAPTER X

Creating Interest and Confidence

HE was a very disappointed man. We had met two days previously when he had been one of the main speakers at the wedding of a mutual friend's daughter. He had proposed the health of the bride's parents. At the wedding he told me that he wanted to come and see me, and we fixed an appointment. Our discussion, when he came to my office, went something like this:

"I didn't think I was so bad," he said. "But my wife said that everyone looked thoroughly bored after I had been speaking for a few minutes. She kept making signs to me, and that made me forget some of the things I wanted to say. I never thought there was much in this speech business—I've done quite a bit of it after all, but I have to make a speech in a couple of weeks' time, so I thought I'd come to see if you could give me any hints."

"Another wedding reception?" I asked.

"Yes," he nodded. "Another one."

"Well, you know," I began, "speaking at a wedding reception is always difficult, because most people have heard it all before. These speeches usually consist of a series of platitudes strung together, and you haven't much alternative but to use them. The important people present want to hear them, but nobody else does. Eulogies which go on for minutes on end do become boring after a time. There are only two kinds of speech that you can make on these occasions. If you can tell a story really well you can keep the audience interested for quite a while—say five minutes. If you have to resort to stock phrases, you know the kind of thing—a wonderful couple—we all love them—we know that they will be like their parents—what a fine example they have been set—well that kind of thing should never last for more than five minutes—three minutes would be better."

He looked quite hurt about this, and I don't think he believed me when I told him that to keep guests at a wedding reception interested for ten minutes is very hard.

"But tell me," he said, "what did you think of my effort?" He had really only come to see me because he wanted to be reassured, but I couldn't reassure him, because his speech had not been a good one.

"What do you suggest I do next time, then?" he asked.

"Without knowing something more about the occasion it is difficult to give you an answer," I said. "But you do want to keep them interested the whole time."

HOLDING INTEREST

Every speech must contain 'interest arousers'. The reason for this is that we all have difficulty in listening even to an outstanding speaker for any length of time. That is why most top-class speakers have their points of interest well spaced throughout the speech; then they know that if interest flags for a few seconds, they can soon revive it.

Obviously, there is no definite dividing line between the steps in a speech, they should flow into each other quite naturally. However, soon after the opening, you should try to say something so interesting that even the most casual member of the audience will want to hear more from you.

A speech is full of high notes and medium notes—I won't say low notes—but one of the high notes must certainly be directly after the opening, when you should *create interest* in your speech. Having spoken your opening sentence, the audience relaxes slightly as they get over your shock opening, or they assimilate your factual remark, or they smile at your informal method of address. But that is the time when your step *creating interest* must come into its own and get the speech really moving.

Here are some ways of winning interest quickly:

Yes—No

If you felt that someone had unjustifiably criticised you, you would like to argue it out with your critic, wouldn't you?

If a statement were completely contrary to your way of thinking, you would like to give your point of view, wouldn't you?

If someone lectured you on your way of life and made what you thought was a definite misstatement right at the beginning, you would want to debate that point . . .

That is what happens when a speaker gets 'NO' responses during his speech. If it happens at the end of a speech it isn't too bad, because you have, at least, been listening to him nearly all the time and have assimilated most of what he has had to say. If, however, the controversial point is raised at the beginning

of the speech—a point which arouses a 'NO' response
in you immediately—then you will find great difficulty
in concentrating on what the speaker has to say afterwards—you will be too angry to listen. You will be
muttering to your neighbours—you will be turning
around to friends and saying, "That's quite wrong!"
This could be a great pity, because you might miss some
of the speaker's vital points which could help him to
prove to you that he is, in fact, right, and you are
wrong. But you are not prepared to listen to his
argument. Once your mind is closed because of
what he has said, then your ears are also deaf to his
words.

Yes, that is what happens with 'NO' responses. A
'NO' response means that members of the audience
want to jump up and shout loudly, "No, you're
wrong!" They can't do this during a speech, so they
bottle it up and that's bad for them and bad for the
speaker.

I began this chapter by telling you about my visitor
who was worried. He spent some time with me, and we
discussed 'NO' responses, but he laughed it all aside
and said that it hardly applied to a wedding-reception
speech anyway. But his speech had, in fact, included
a 'NO' response, although that is most unusual in a
speech of that nature.

Here is a little background to that wedding reception. The father of the bride is a great welfare worker
and at the reception were many of his friends, as well
as people whom he had helped. Some of them had
come from one of the poorest districts in London,
where he carried on his good work. And this is what
my visitor had said, soon after his opening remark:

"X. has dedicated his life to the people of B. . . . He has lived among them, among the sordidness and unhappiness . . ."

I felt the 'NO' response to that immediately—and so did others near to me. Many of those people were poor, yes. Parts of their neighbourhood were sordid. But the majority of them were not all that unhappy—in fact, some of them were very happy.

If, then, it is possible to get a 'NO' response under the ideal conditions of a wedding-reception speech, every speaker ought to watch out for this on more difficult occasions.

During a speech dealing with the rearmament of Germany a speaker, within the first few seconds, started deriding a book written by Lord Russell. He created a big 'NO' response among many people in his audience. A number of them would have liked to have argued the point.

This does not mean that a speaker must not be controversial. A controversial speech can be most stimulating. But an audience does want to listen to reasoned arguments before the major point of controversy arises.

A speaker should not have his audience violently disagreeing with him before he has got under way. After all, in nearly every controversy there are some points about which there can be a common agreement, and these should be voiced early in the speech.

But, you may ask, what has all this got to do with creating interest?

If you take the opposite to the 'NO' response, and you say something which will get a 'YES' response, then you are using the best means of creating interest quickly.

We don't want to be treated like sheep when we are members of an audience, but we do like to feel that the speaker is seeing our point of view as he would like us to see his.

Here are some of the thoughts which go through our mind when a speaker gets a 'YES' response:

He's got a good point there.
There's a lot in that.
Yes, that's fair enough.
Well, I won't disagree with that.

When a speaker gets a 'YES' response, therefore, he not only interests the audience, but he makes them feel important, and we become more interested when we feel important.

A salesman sells by getting 'YES' responses throughout his sale. He knows that if there is an argument, it is always the buyer who will win. He also knows that if he says anything which gets a 'NO' response, it becomes almost impossible to persuade the buyer to change his mind.

When we are members of an audience the speaker will find it just as impossible to get us to change our minds if he gets a 'NO' response.

Here, then, is a certain way of creating interest from the very beginning of the speech. Say something which you know will get the audience to agree with you.

The best way to create interest is to get a 'YES' response.

Off the Record

A good way of creating interest early in a speech is by giving some off-the-record information, if that is possible. We all like to know what goes on behind the scenes at a Government debate, a board meeting, a selection board, or at the theatre. Very little information is given in this way which will not quickly become public knowledge, but it does help to create our interest, even if we know that it is of little account.

Exhibits

If your speech lends itself to the showing of an exhibit early in the speech, then you have a certain way of getting interest soon after the commencement.

What Interests You

What is your main interest right now? This book? That's very kind of you, but you are only interested in this book inasmuch as you think it may be of help to you. Perhaps I am right in assuming that your main interests are in your family, yourself, your business, your hobbies . . .

The same applies to your audiences. If I meet YOU, and I speak about YOU, YOUR FAMILY, YOUR BUSINESS, or YOUR HOBBIES, then you will be interested in what I have to say.

When you meet your audiences you are certain of being interesting to them if you think on those lines.

If you are going to talk about their hobbies, then start right away by creating interest. Tell them how you can help them

This, of course, is the YOU-WE-I formula again—but you will see this referred to constantly in this book. It is something worth repeating over and over again. We feel that it is so important that at our Courses we give

every member attending a small token on which is
printed

YOU-WE-I

so that it will be a constant reminder when speaking,
to think in terms of the other person's interests.

CREATING CONFIDENCE

Do you know anything about me? In spite of the
fact that in the last few years I have written fourteen
books of various kinds, that one of my companies
advertises extensively under my name, and that we
train men for hundreds of the leading companies in
this country, the chances are that until you picked up
this book you had never heard of me.

If, then, you were to invite me to speak at, say, your
association meeting or at the opening of a charitable
appeal, the majority of the audience would want to
know what right I had to call myself an expert on
a particular subject, or why I should have been
accorded the honour of making the appeal.

A good chairman should cover this ground, but the
majority do not help a speaker a great deal. An audience wants to have confidence in a speaker, and if
he is unknown to them it is quite in order for him,
in his opening remarks, to give a few facts about himself.

You may well remind me now of the YOU-WE-I
formula. This is one of the very few occasions
when you may reverse it. But the point must not be
stressed.

Provided the speaker talks modestly and briefly

about himself, and brings the step into the speech in a natural and pleasing manner, most of the audience will be pleased to hear the news that the speaker knows his job.

Don't forget, even after-dinner speakers use this step. When a speaker says, "I have known Joe Bloggs for forty-six years . . ." he is only telling the audience that they can have confidence in his judgment of Joe Bloggs because he has known him for such a long time.

Whatever you do, don't go to the extreme of listing your achievements. Just a short oblique reference will do. For example:

> "Those six years spent under Ferguson in Ecuador taught me a great deal . . ."
>
> "As I started at the bench I know how many of you may be feeling . . ."
>
> "Soon after the *Bird Life* book I wrote was published, I had an amusing letter . . ."
>
> "There have, of course, been many improvements since 1924 when I first designed . . ."

The sales manager of one of our leading cigarette manufacturers told me that he always advises his salesmen that they must never rely on the name of their company to create confidence. He says to them, "You must create confidence yourself at every call."

If a representative of a large concern, who knows his customers, has to be reminded to create confidence, then surely it must be of importance to a speaker who may be little known to his audience.

This step does not apply to those who are well known

to members of the audience. To the majority of speakers, however, it is well worth while including.

NOW REFER TO YOUR SPEECH ON THE WELFARE STATE AND CHECK ON THE FIRST THREE STEPS. POLISH UP IF NECESSARY.

CHAPTER XI

The Body of the Speech

SOME time ago a comedian, Milton Hayes, won a good reputation for himself by making a fifteen-minute speech at each of his performances. That was his act. He hardly uttered a coherent sentence—the whole thing didn't make sense—yet it was all highly entertaining. Perhaps, when we saw him we thought of the dozens of speakers we had heard and not understood. Alternatively, he may have filled a psychological need. Perhaps we should all like to talk nonsense on occasion.

His act would go something like this: *Good evening friends and—er—those who believe that the entertainment by films—yes, I must say this with all sincerity and all the strength I can—er—that the—er—the preference—and without any hesitation climb down most firmly—and I must say this with vigour and the type of—er—student who—and all this has nothing to do but to row with the best of them, and while shouldering that responsibility . . .*

I bet you didn't even smile. Written down it isn't even worth reading, and yet Milton Hayes made an act of it. Yes, we all laughed at his gibberish. We didn't have to sit back and smile as though we understood what he was saying when we hadn't the slightest idea what it was all about.

And that brings us to the gibberish part of the speech—the main theme.

In spite of what I have written on speech-building, in spite of the fact that many speakers do build their speeches, something seems to happen to them when they are on their feet, and they begin to jump from point to point, to add to their speech—and that is where the gibberish commences. Many speakers open well. A high percentage of them hold our interest. If, for a moment, we leave out the centre of the speech we can say that many speakers close well. It is during the main theme that they go astray.

Here is a major point: You must divide your main theme into several steps. You must treat each step as a speech in itself, with an opening (main sentence), a middle and an end (the lead into the next step). Having divided all your main steps, NEVER ALTER THEM ONCE YOU HAVE COMMENCED SPEAKING. If you do —if you feel that the applause is of such a nature that you must do more justice to your cause, if you believe that the audience want to hear more—you stand a good chance of becoming another Milton Hayes, but under the wrong conditions.

Constantly, throughout this book, I have referred to the YOU appeal, and you must continue with this when you build up your main theme. What is it that the audience WANT from you? Find that out—fill the want, and you will make a good speech.

Let us list the major *wants* of most audiences:

To learn something.
To gain money.
To feel sentimental.
To feel pleased.
To benefit health.
To have love and affection.
To feel proud.
Self-preservation.

Amusement.

Faith.

There may be other *wants*, but these cover most of the ground. Think it out for yourself, and see if you can find any others.

Assuming that you have six steps in your main theme, then you have to try to fill one want with each step. Here are some examples:

A Speech to Heating and Ventilating Contractors on Electrostatic Precipitation for Dust Collecting
  Six main steps—
    four steps *to learn*
    one step—*self-preservation* (if they don't advise electrostatic precipitation someone else will)
    one step—*pride* (pride in installations completed).

A Speech to Members of a Women's Institute On How They Can Help to Bring About Hygiene in Food Shops
  Four main steps—
    one step—*self-preservation*
    one step—*to benefit health*
    two steps—*to learn* (how they can help to bring about results).

A Speech By a Managing Director to Members of His Staff on Success
  Six main steps—
    one step—*to learn*
    two steps—*to gain money*
    one step—*sentiment*
    one step—*self-preservation*
    one step—*faith* (in the managing director's desire to help them).

If you check each of your steps in a speech with the *wants* you will be able to see that they have YOU appeal.

THE WANTS

This is how you can apply these wants to any speech you make:

To Learn

Have you ever listened to a speaker hoping to learn something, and been disappointed at the result? That is because the speaker did not check the *want* list. Possibly, he thought you wanted amusement, so he told too many stories. Possibly, he thought that you would want to feel proud of his achievements, when you only wanted to feel proud of the fact that you were trying to master a new subject.

If the audience *wants* to learn something from you, then the majority of your main steps must be covered by the *want*: *to learn*.

In the example I gave of the speech to the heating and ventilating contractors, the contractors obviously wanted to learn, and so the speaker devoted about seventy per cent of his time to teaching, and thirty per cent to driving home the fact that his lessons must be put into practice *for their own benefit*.

The speaker at the Women's Institute only devoted fifty per cent to learning, because the majority of those present would, of course, know what action to take, i.e. avoiding dirty shops, asking for wrapped goods, suggesting to shop owners how they could instruct staff in hygiene, etc. He wanted to advise them to do something about it, so he aroused the *want*: *self-preservation*. He insisted that they should take these precautions, and take action, for the safety of their children and their families. His next step dealt with benefits to health; pointing out that they would stand less chance of food poisoning if they took the trouble to see that the shops were run on more hygienic lines; and so he covered the ground adequately.

It is usually only a lecturer on a specific subject who can devote all of his main steps to teaching or to filling the *want*: *to learn*. Even he would do well to try to bring in one or two other *wants* if, by so doing, he could make his speech more interesting to the audience.

To Gain Money

If a speaker can help us to increase our incomes then he is, indeed, welcome. Some speakers who are able to do this, however, only refer to the subject obliquely. Even the speaker on electrostatic precipitation might have put in an extra step pointing out to the contractors that it would help them to increase their profits.

This *want* should be carefully studied by all speakers who address employees. Those who talk to salesmen, others who try to get production increased, must not get away from the fact that the main reason for the audience wanting to listen to them is not because they want to be able to sell more or to produce more, but because they want to *earn more*.

Many Government speakers talk on the need for increased exports. They, naturally, all stress the fact

that the country must export to live; that the various
Government departments help in no small measure;
that it is better to send salesmen abroad than to try
to deal with the matters by post—but not many
speakers stress the *gain of money*.

I did hear this point mentioned by a Government
speaker recently, and he got rounds of applause, everyone beaming agreement. He said, "And here is the
main reason why you should fight for exports: It will
bring you extra profits, and although we shall take
most of it back (laughter) there will still be a lot left
for you."

The listeners—mostly business executives—appreciated this down-to-earth talk, because we all become
a little tired of platitudes.

Sentiment

It does us all good to feel sentimental on occasion.
Just one step only in the main body of the speech
devoted to *sentiment* can be greatly appreciated by an
audience. This can be in the form of a tribute to someone—someone who has done good work for a club or
an association—someone who, perhaps, has been too
ill to come to the meeting.

M. Herriot in his speech to the Assembly on E.D.C.
said, "I am an old man, at the end of my life . . ." He
was appealing to sentiment.

Wilfred Pickles in an appeal told the story of an old
couple living out their days together on a pittance, who
refused to part with their fox-terrier. He was appealing
to our sentiment.

Always check this *want*, but use it only when it can
be used sincerely.

THE BODY OF THE SPEECH

Pleasure

We all like to feel pleased—particularly with ourselves. When an audience can be congratulated on having achieved something, then this step can give pleasure.

Good news—a well-recited poem—an extract from a poem—a well-turned phrase—all can give pleasure to varying audiences. They are good ingredients for this step.

For a speaker to tell a story of achievement can give pleasure. That is the only other occasion when the YOU-WE-I formula can be reversed.

We can identify ourselves with the speaker as he tells us how he made difficult headway up that glacier, or how he fought his way through a swampy jungle . . .

We also feel pleased at a tribute paid to someone which we should like to pay but have called upon the speaker to voice for us.

To Benefit Health

"If you relax, your health will benefit."

That is a main step in a talk I have given over and over again on relaxing. For years I did not mention this. Most of the speech was devoted to the art of relaxing, and how it helps to overcome nervous tension in speakers. When I discovered that it did benefit health—then I made it a separate step.

So many people seem to be worried about their health these days, that if you can use a step in your speech which will help to benefit their health, you will be well rewarded by the interest shown.

To Have Love and Affection

Many speakers on marriage guidance and all speakers talking about family affairs use this step. *How to achieve love and affection* is certain to arouse the deepest interest. The same applies to matters relating to sex.

If a speaker is dealing with these subjects he must be adult, and not boggle at the thought of speaking to a mixed audience. If he can help them with their sex life, or help them *to achieve love and affection*, then this step must be included.

Pride

Pride in the achievement of others—*pride* in our community—*pride* in our country—*pride* in our organisation . . . Yes, we like to feel *proud* of something.

And that feeling of *pride* can be engendered by many speakers to the benefit of the audience—and to their own benefit as well.

Self-Preservation

With this step can be coupled our *sense of caution*. We listen to speakers on Civil Defence because *self-preservation* is a natural part of our make-up—especially as we grow older.

Amusement

Yes, we *want* to be *amused* on less serious occasions, and even during a serious speech a little light relief can actually help to impress on us the more vital points at issue.

You may well think that a speaker talking on a light matter is continually causing *amusement* by his anecdotes and quotations. True, but this need not stop him from devoting a whole step to an *amusing* story which drives home a point in the speech.

Faith

This is a difficult subject to touch upon, and I shall not deal with its religious implications.

If a speaker can help just one member of an audience to have more *faith* in himself, *faith* in his country, *faith* in his work, then he should use that step in his speech.

Deal with as many *wants* as you can, and you will make a good speech.

NOW REFER TO YOUR SPEECH ON THE
WELFARE STATE AND CHECK UP ON
THE BODY OF THE SPEECH.

CHAPTER XII

Closing the Speech

BUD FLANAGAN, the famous comedian, had kindly invited me to spend a few evenings backstage at the Victoria Palace. At the time I was writing a book with a stage background. Knowing little about what went on behind the footlights, I was grateful for the invitation.

I couldn't have spent a more enjoyable week. The Crazy Gang were just as funny in the wings and dressing-rooms as they were on the stage. During the show Bud Flanagan had sung a song which was a smash hit. One night the applause was even more deafening than usual. The number of encores had, of course, been laid down, and obviously the time-table did not lend itself to any additions. For all that, several people in the wings were saying, "Give 'em just one more, Bud." "No," he answered, "they'll all be happier wanting more. Let the show go on," or words to that effect.

There is a lesson in that for every public speaker. Once he has decided on his close he must stick to it, and not continue just because the audience looks as though it is enjoying his performance.

Don't Give Closing Signals

It is always easy to recognise the speaker who has not studied the fundamentals of his job. He begins by apologising and ends with a warning—a warning to the audience that he is about to finish.

That wouldn't be so bad if he were to keep to his promise.

He rarely does.

The nervous speaker invariably gives closing signals. Here is a selection of them:

> "And finally I must tell you . . ."
> "My speech is coming to its close . . ."
> "Here is a final story . . ."
> "Before I sit down I must tell you . . ."
> "One last word . . ."
> "In conclusion . . ."
> "No doubt you have heard enough of me, well I am about to finish now, but . . ."

These are all closing signals. Never give them. The reason why they are used by nervous speakers is because throughout the speech they are longing for the end, and it gives them great encouragement when they can say with an air of finality, "And now I am about to finish . . ." But then a strange thing happens. Once having said that, their confidence returns. They know they can sit down whenever they like, and they begin to feel happy. They begin to enjoy the speech. Instead, then, of finishing and sitting down, they go on talking. They think of all the things they wanted to speak about and which they were too nervous to introduce earlier, and they tell them.

Remember, don't give a closing signal, but when you do decide to close—finish.

Surprise

Far better than warning the audience that the speech is ending, is to take them by surprise. Let them feel that you are still in full sail, that there is a lot more of the speech to come—then end suddenly.

You will not startle them. You will please them with the way you have finished—provided you use one of the standard closing techniques.

CLOSING TECHNIQUES

If you prepare a first-class close to suit your speech your ending will satisfy the whole audience.

The Summary Close

This is a particularly useful close if you want the audience to remember the salient features of your speech long after you have finished talking.

You conclude by summarising the main points, but you don't warn them of the fact—otherwise you will be giving closing signals. You wouldn't finish by saying, "Now let me summarise . . ." But you might say, "You will remember that . . ." and then give your points.

Here is an example:

Speech on Police Recruiting

"On the welfare side there is every opportunity to enjoy a favourite sport. The pay is good. The duties of the man on the beat are interesting and varied. Uniformed constables can do spells of duty as plain-clothes men helping the C.I.D. In other words, it is a first-rate career." (*end*)

Another example:

Speech on House Magazines

"Just think for a moment what can be achieved. It helps to create and maintain goodwill. It creates enthusiasm. It helps to increase production and sales. It benefits and pleases your customers. It keeps your shareholders in the picture. It saves a great deal of correspondence because new developments can be fully explained in such a magazine. It helps your export agents. That, I think, is all the proof you need that you should develop a house magazine." (*end*)

The Question Close

It is sometimes a good thing for a speaker to let his audience go away trying to think of the answer to a definite question he has put to them.

If it is put to them early in the speech they tend to forget it. When the speaker concludes with a question, however, they remember it.

This is how it can be used:

Speech at a Shareholders' Meeting of an Hotel Group

"It is a question of going either backwards or forwards. Our patrons are loyal, but until we modernise our West End premises we are not going to make the number of new customers which is so vital to us if we are to progress. The capital required is not small I know, but we must find it. The suggested new preference shares, about which I told you, will carry an eight per cent dividend. The question you must ask yourselves is: Can you do better with your money? I don't think you can." (*end*)

Speech on Keeping London Litter-Free

"Much has been done already, but we still have a long way to go before we can approach the cleanliness of those continental cities I mentioned earlier. The new ideas I have outlined will do a great deal to help, but it is vital to have the co-operation of everyone who wants to see this lovely town of ours looking spick and span. The question we all have to ask ourselves is: How can we make London the tidiest city in the world?" (*end*)

The Dramatic Close

The *dramatic close* is rarely used, but it can be effective on occasion.

This is how it is explained by A. C. Hazel in *Professional Salesmanship*:

"The dramatic ending can often be most effective. I still remember an old professor who on certain occasions used to use the dramatic type of ending to his address. Towards the end of his talk he would appeal to us students and say that if we had not understood the points he had been putting over and if we did not appreciate the importance of his subject, then—he would slump dramatically in his chair—he was a failure. Our reaction to this type of ending was that we felt that we could not let this poor old man down, and much effort was made to try to remember what he had been putting over.

"Another effective trick is to lower the voice gradually, until it is almost a whisper, and then sit down. The reverse technique is also equally effective, namely, to raise the voice to a crescendo, and then sit down." (*end*)

Closing with a Poem or Quotation

If you are proud of your voice and diction and if you can recite poetry, a *poetic close* can be used effectively by you on occasion.

So far as a quotation is concerned, you can only end with a quotation if it sums up your whole speech.

A good *poetic close* was the following, used by a speaker proposing the toast: *The Ladies.*

> *Where is the man who has the power and skill*
> *To stem the torrent of a woman's will?*
> *For if she will, she will, you may depend on't;*
> *And if she won't, she won't; so there's an end on't.*

A strong *quotation close* was used by a speaker on intemperance. He concluded:

"To drink or not to drink is a voluntary choice· As Seneca said: *Drunkenness is nothing but voluntary madness.*"

The opposite to this was the speaker who spoke on wine. He extolled the virtues of the grape, and concluded:

"Besides this it is also good for your health. After all, it was the great Louis Pasteur who said: *Wine is the most healthful and most hygienic of all beverages.* Let us always drink it then, for our pleasure and for our health."

The Concession Close

Can you give away anything? Can you grant a concession? It isn't often that a speaker can make use of this close, but if it so happens that you can use it, you will do well to do so.

Here is an example:

> *Speech at a Meeting to Discuss Final Arrangements Regarding the Formation of a New Club*
>
> "You now have all the facts before you, and I am sure you will agree that the provisional committee have done a splendid job. The committee, as you know, feel that we must ask for an entrance fee of £25 and an annual subscription of ten guineas. But here is an important point: Everyone who decides to join us to-day can become a founder member for only £40. This will make them life members, with no further amounts to be paid at any time. Gentlemen, it's up to you to take advantage of this." (*end*)

The Story Close

The *story close* appeals if the stories are good. The stories can be of a serious nature or they can be humorous. If you can end by having the audience laughing, then you will have succeeded in closing your speech on the right note. If your anecdote is so interesting that they are absorbed by it up to the last second, then once again your task will have been well accomplished.

Here are some examples:

Speech at a Travel Association Meeting

"Some years ago a young man, his wife and two children arrived at Victoria Station from the Continent. He had little money and didn't know London, but he did have an address to go to in the suburbs. As he stood on the pavement with his family, surrounded by luggage, he wondered how he was to get to his destination. The last bus had gone. A cab pulled up and the driver asked if he could be of assistance. In broken English the young man explained where he wanted to go, and the family got into the cab. When they arrived at the address he had given he found, to his horror, that his purse with the little money it contained was gone. He tried to explain the position to the cabby, who told him not to worry. 'Leave it till you're settled in, and take this to help,' he said, and handed over a £1 note before he drove off.

"This is a true story. I cannot think of a better example of kindliness and courtesy to foreign visitors. It is rare to meet a case where help is needed of this kind, but as long as we remember that these visitors from abroad are our guests, and show them courtesy and friendship, then our tourist trade is bound to grow." (*end*)

As an example of the *humorous story* ending, this was used by the speaker at a Luncheon Club:

"A short while ago I made what I thought was a very good speech. Feeling the need of a little praise, I asked a friend afterwards for his opinion of my effort. 'A good speech,' he told me, 'a very good speech. But you missed several fine opportunities of sitting down.' Well, I won't miss this one." (*end*)

And with that he sat down, amidst applause.

To Salesmen Representing Manufacturers of Vacuum Cleaners

"When I was young and very raw to the game, I canvassed Billington—that's a little village in Devon, umpteen miles from anywhere. I knocked at the door of a cottage, and an old man opened it and asked me what he could do for me. I told him, in the fifteen hundred set words we had to use in those days, and when I had finished he said, 'No good, lad, I've got a carpet sweeper.' I thought of stock answer number twelve and with a beam on my face said, 'That's wonderful, sir, now I can really help you. I'll make the most generous allowance if you will have one of these new models.' 'Can't do that, lad,' he answered slowly, 'I must stick by my bargain—after all, I picked her for better or worse.'

When the laughter had died down he added, "Well, you've had me for better or for worse. I hope you feel it was for the better." (*end*)

Fear Close

When a speaker wants to frighten us into taking his advice, he uses a *fear close*.

Here are examples:

A Speech to Help Collect Funds for a Youth Club

"You have heard what has happened to three young people in this village within a period of twelve months. Are we going to sit back smugly and say that these were exceptional cases? There can't be one person in this hall who will not bear me out when I say that every night of the week our young people are to be seen lounging about at street corners. And when boys and girls have nothing to do they look for trouble. I don't mean bad children—I don't believe there are many bad children, but even good ones can become bad when they are idle, as we all know. We must have this club, and I ask you to dig deep into your pockets to save our children, or your boy may go the way of Robert ——." (*end*)

Speech at Trade Meeting to Discuss Price Cutting

"In our business we have, over the years, all striven to improve the service we give to our customers. But, as I said earlier, good service costs money, and if we cut the margin of profit on our goods, we cannot maintain our high standards. These price cutters say they are bringing down the cost of living, but they don't mean it. All they are concerned with is the sale of their goods—not in looking after their customers. We know that we cannot afford to sell cheaper, and neither can they in the long run. I ask you to agree with me that this Association takes immediate action to stop these people from attempting to ruin our livelihood. If we don't do something quickly, we shan't have any business to worry about." (*end*)

The Alternative Close

As the heading implies, the speaker leaves his audience with two *alternative* lines of action from which to choose.

Here are some examples:

Speech at a Political Meeting

"No, ladies and gentlemen, it is not just a question of more money and less work for everybody. The facts are perfectly clear. Britain has made great headway in the last few years for the same reason as she has made progress for generation after generation: Her people are still basically good craftsmen and honest workers. But we have had a heavy burden to carry, and the cost to our programme has been a high one. Nevertheless, our party has not made idle promises. We have fulfilled our obligations. Think of this: Are you going to take a chance now on untried methods, or are you going to continue to progress under the guidance of a party which has kept its word?" (*end*)

Speech at a Meeting of Executives to Discuss Increased Production to Capture Export Markets

"As the previous speaker has said, world markets are hardening and the question of mass production is becoming of great importance. If we cannot increase the size of our factories—if we cannot obtain more skilled workers, then new machinery, new production methods must take their place. Prices must be brought down to fight increasing competition. You have to decide whether to continue to produce fewer quality goods at a high price, or to introduce mass production techniques, to enable you greatly to increase the sales by quoting lower prices. Which will you do?" (*end*)

Action Close

You want *action*. You want the audience to do something and to do it quickly. Then you use an *action close*. Here is one:

An Appeal for Help to Preserve a Local Beauty Spot

"Five alternative claims have been put forward to the Council and the Government department concerned, and they are all equally suitable. Somebody, somewhere, some bureaucrat ensconced in his miserable department, says 'No'. This beautiful village green of ours, with centuries of tradition behind it, must go, otherwise it will mean an alteration in plans made by people who haven't even had the decency to come here and find out for themselves what it means to us. We cannot—we will not allow it. A petition has been drawn up, and Mr. Mason is going to present it personally to our Member of Parliament. We want your signatures—and we want them now— not in a day or so, or the day after to-morrow— not even to-morrow, but before you leave this hall. Mr. Burgen has it waiting for you to sign. He is standing by the exit—sign before you leave." (*end*)

SOME MORE EXAMPLES

Now you must provide yourself with some more examples. Read through the various closes again and again, until you thoroughly understand their implications. Then work out for each of the following speeches four different kinds of close:

On Stamp Collecting.

On National Society for Prevention of Cruelty to
    Children.
Do Monopolies Cause Increased Prices?
How to Enjoy Opera.
Crime Does Not Pay.
Winston Churchill.
Abraham Lincoln.

AFTER IT'S ALL OVER

When you have finished your speech and you are
left with your thoughts, ask yourself these questions:

Did I interest them?
Did I bore them?
Did I irritate them?
Did I answer the questions they had in mind?
Was I sincere?
Was I enthusiastic?

If you can answer these questions correctly, you
will have made a good speech.

> CHECK UP ON THE CLOSE YOU USED
> FOR YOUR SPEECH ON THE WELFARE
> STATE AND SEE IF IT NEEDS POLISHING
> UP.

CHAPTER XIII

The Length of the Speech

HAVE you ever heard of a *listenometer*? No? I hope you will at some time in the future. I should very much like to invent one. It will save endless trouble.

It will be a machine which, when fitted in a room in which a speech is being made, will advise the speaker as to the number of seconds or minutes when members of the audience are not listening to him. Of course, it will have to be able to read their minds to do this, and that is a bit of a problem. It will only switch itself on when their minds start to wander.

It will be useful in general conversation as well. Imagine how it will assist the salesman—a click—a glance—he will realise that the customer is not listening to him, and therefore he will have to do something to liven matters up . . . It would show amazing results. It would make me realise that I talk too much (most people are too kind to remind me of this!) and it would help others in the same way.

Men always believe that women never stop talking. That's unfair. Men are just as bad. What we mean is that when we arrive home in the evening we have done our talking, and as we don't listen much during the day, we don't want to have to listen much when we get home at night.

We should all be a lot wiser—yes, and better public speakers, too—if we were to decide to talk less and listen more, and when talking in public to cut all our speeches in half.

Twenty-four years ago I was given this advice, and it's the best advice that can be given to a public speaker. Whenever you are asked to speak, and have been allocated time for it—cut down that time. When you are not given any time limit to adhere to—don't speak for more than ten minutes. All I will add to that is: Sometimes five minutes is better than ten.

The only exception to this rule is when a lecture is to be given. This may have to fill in half an hour or an hour, but we shall deal with that under the chapter dealing with lectures.

After-dinner speakers are the worst offenders. They invariably talk too much. Time passes quickly for the speaker—he is probably enjoying himself—but it drags so for the guests.

Look at it in this way: A first-class entertainer rarely has an act lasting longer than ten minutes. There are only a handful of exceptions and even they can only command our attention for half an hour or so when they are right at the top of their form. Ten minutes is all that we can take from a top entertainer—yet we think that we can entertain for longer. Foolish, isn't it? A short speech is rarely a bad speech.

Time Keeping

If you are given a time limit, cut it down if you can, but if you can't, NEVER RUN OVER YOUR TIME. You may be told by the sponsors of a meeting that they would like you to talk on your pet subject for forty minutes. Try to make it thirty minutes, and let another speaker fill in the gap if necessary; or let the audience have a longer break. Have a clock or watch in front of you, and if you find that you have ten minutes of a speech left but only five minutes of time, CUT YOUR SPEECH. If you don't like having a watch or clock in front of you, ask the chairman to pass a note to you telling you when you have only a few minutes left. This may be done so surreptitiously that no-one will notice. If you must talk for forty-five minutes, then you must have visual aids with which to hold the interest of your audience.

Watch for Them

We cannot make a hundred-per-cent-effective-speech on every occasion. That is our aim, but sometimes, in spite of the fact that a speech has been carefully prepared, or is prepared to a plan, step by step, there are passages which are not so interesting as they might be.

During your speech you can check this by looking at the audience. Watch them for signs of boredom. These signs are:

One yawn may not matter—six yawns mean boredom.

When they look at the ceiling, apparently watching flies at work, they are bored.

When they talk amongst themselves, they are bored.

When a noise outside the building interests them more than your speech, then they are bored.

When they look at their watches frequently, they are bored.

These are distress signals. When you see them, CUT YOUR SPEECH SHORT.

To All Executives

There should be a society formed for the prevention of mental cruelty to staff by directors. A director, when he addresses his staff, knows that they must listen . . . they must show interest . . . they must applaud . . . they must stay to the end.

Whether it is because of this or not I don't know, but invariably ALL executives talk too long. Staff lectures are generally appreciated, provided they are cut short.

A Golden Rule

Write down your speech. Check it for interesting points. Make certain that you have a good interest point at frequent intervals. See that the subject matter which builds up each step is interesting. Check on your anecdotes and historical references and your quotation . . .

NOW CUT YOUR SPEECH, and you are bound to be successful.

CHAPTER XIV

Confidence Cards Never Let You Down

HE had only a few words to say. He had probably rehearsed them for weeks. They should have been simple enough to remember, they were: "The car has broken down." His part in the play was a small one—in fact this was the only line he had to speak, as he came on in the first act, and did not appear again.

One would think that he would not even have to rehearse such a line, but no doubt he did rehearse thoroughly. Possibly, he felt that the part was quite an important one and, if he could give it enough emphasis, some owner-producer watching the show might realise his ability, and so would begin another rise to stardom.

In spite of rehearsals, in spite of the fact that there were only five words in the line, he didn't speak it correctly on the opening night.

I saw that happen. You must have seen the same kind of thing happen yourself. If you are a regular television viewer then you have undoubtedly seen it occur over and over again. If, then, it is possible for an actor, who should have a good memory, to forget a line on occasion, obviously a public speaker would find it hard to memorise a speech word by word.

There is no need for you to worry about this. Many speakers do spend hours rehearsing their part, making their speech over and over again, trying to make themselves word-perfect. Far better for them to adopt a simple technique which will enable them to use notes in such a manner that, even if their mind becomes completely blank, they will still, after a quick reference to a card, be able to carry on.

This is not just theory. It has been proved effective over a number of years by many speakers. Before I tell you about our Confidence Cards, which form the basis of this plan, let us think about the kind of speech you may be called upon to make.

(i) You can read your speech.

(ii) You can make an extemporaneous or impromptu speech.

(iii) You can prepare your speech, and work from notes.

Reading a Speech

Generally, a speaker only reads a speech when he has been asked to lecture, or when the speech is to be reported, and it is essential, therefore, for it to be accurate. Few speeches which are read are enjoyed. They sound monotonous and the audience become so tired of looking at the top of the speaker's head as he bends down to read his paper. Also, they become a little irritated when words pour from him like a torrent —words which he has obviously memorised—and then suddenly he dries up, as he realises that he must return to his brief for help.

It is true that a speech which is read can be a more polished speech than an extemporaneous one. The speaker can spend a lot of time rewording phrases until they are perfect, but unless he can read extremely well, even his rhetoric will sound dull.

How many people can read aloud? If a person cannot read a book aloud effectively, then how can he be expected to read a speech enthusiastically?

If you are called upon to read a speech, then you must set about it in the right way. You must begin by practising reading from a book. You should spend a half-hour each day doing this; it will enable you to get the right inflections in your voice. It should help you to alter your voice to line up with the passages you are reading. It will help you to give light and shade to the text. More important still, practice will enable you to take in one or two lines ahead, so that you will be able to look at the audience now and again.

When you feel that you are competent, then you can read your own speech, which you have written out, and this should be read aloud as many times as possible before the big day arrives.

It is hard work reading a speech—avoid it if you can.

Never, in any circumstances, attempt to read a speech when there is no necessity to do so.

The Impromptu or Extemporaneous Speech

I am an inefficient impromptu speaker, and that is why I rarely speak in this manner. On occasions when, at meetings, I have been asked to speak, if I have not formed any strong views about the subject under discussion I usually tell the chairman that I have no other ideas to place before the meeting than those already given. I advise you to adopt this attitude also.

If ever I have made a good (apparently) impromptu speech, then it has not really been impromptu at all.

That is not being unfair to anyone. If you do this it only means that before attending a meeting or a dinner where you have an idea that you might be

called upon to speak, you have given some consideration to what you intend to say. If, then, there is the
remotest chance of your being called upon to say something in public, do make some provision in advance.
If you don't speak you will not have wasted much
time, because you need not build a complete speech.
All that you should do is to concentrate on one thought
only—one aspect of the problem which is going to be
discussed. Then, if you are called upon to speak, you
can deal with that one aspect—and deal with it
efficiently.

Prepare Your Speech and Work from Notes

This speech is one which you have carefully thought
out before it is delivered. You have written it out and,
possibly, partly memorised some of the passages. Because, however, you have not committed the whole
speech to memory, you are at liberty to develop it
along any lines you wish.

The result is that the speech sounds natural and live.
You don't have to concentrate on whole passages
which you have tried to memorise, and you are able
to deliver your speech in a most effective manner.

This can be the ideal speech.

WORKING TO A PLAN

How, then, are you going to remember your speech?
You can:

Write it out fully and read it.
Write it out fully and memorise it.
Write it out fully and refer to your papers during
the speech.

Write out notes to which you can refer during the speech.

Write it out fully and memorise the headings.

Write It Out Fully and Read It

This we have already discussed, and my advice is: Don't do it.

Write It Out Fully and Memorise It

But can you do this? If you have such a fine memory that you can memorise a whole speech without any trouble, then you are a fortunate person, and you should be a good speaker. You will be able to polish every phrase, and having rehearsed it, you will deliver your speech effectively.

Few of us can do this. An actor might, but so often actors, when making speeches, look as though they are acting. You don't want to give that impression.

However, if you can memorise a whole speech, then make good use of this blessing.

Write It Out Fully and Refer To It

This can never be effective. To try to read each word from typewritten or handwritten pages—or even from a paper on which the words are printed in large letters—is most difficult. If you attempt to do this you will lose your place, you will become worried, and you will make a bad speech.

Write Out Notes to Which You Can Refer

This is quite a normal procedure, and it often works well, provided the notes are legible and can be understood by the speaker. If we have a bad memory, a few words written down, the meaning of which were quite clear when we were preparing our speech, may mean nothing to us when we are actually on our feet, speaking. Notes written on a foolscap sheet of paper help at the beginning of the speech, but a speaker may lose his place and not find it easy to follow his notes because of this.

Write It Out Fully and Memorise the Headings

This, we have found, is easily the best policy for a speaker. But merely to write the headings is not sufficient. That is similar to making notes.

The headings must convey to the speaker the step with which he is dealing, and the subject matter which he is going to use during that step.

This can be achieved by writing out a good sentence to lead in to a step in the speech.

SENTENCES

First write out your speech in full. Then look for your key points—your opening, creation of interest, creation of confidence, the six or eight steps in the body of the speech, the close. Underline the main sentences leading in to each of these key points. Now polish up those sentences. Keep thinking about them day after day. How can you improve them? Check with your dictionary. Check with your Roget's *Thesaurus* or a similar work. Polish, and polish again.

One of the reasons why I advocate the sentence technique as against using headings as reminders is because it enables a speaker to use a few scintillating sentences.

It takes Sir Winston Churchill to be able to write sentence after sentence, each one a collector's gem—masterpieces of English—epigrams which could only be thought out by a man of outstanding ability. We must be satisfied with perhaps half a dozen good sentences—as good as we can make them—perfect in style and quality, to delight our audiences.

Think about these key sentences. Develop them. You can also develop subsidiary sentences if you wish.

We derive great pleasure from public speaking, as we learn more and more of our language, and begin to appreciate the beauty of the words we use.

Associating Ideas

If we are not to read the speech in full or to memorise it, then headings or sentences must act as our guide. They must remind us of the text to follow.

It doesn't make a great deal of difference whether you work to our plan by using headings or by using polished sentences. I have given you my reasons for preferring the latter.

For example, you might say:

". . . And then the age of heroism, adventure, glory—the Elizabethan era."

That could be a main sentence—a lead-in sentence. Instantly, it would convey to you that part of your speech in which you wish to deal with the battles of Drake, the discoveries of Raleigh, and the greatness of good Queen Bess herself. But if you didn't wish to use this sentence, then the heading would merely be: Elizabethan era.

No doubt this would remind you of what you had

to say. Or would you hesitate on looking at the heading? Would it convey to you all the brilliant sentences with which you intend to follow on? This you will have to think out for yourself. We sent out a questionnaire to a number of speakers, and the result was very nearly fifty-fifty—fifty-four per cent used sentences, forty-six per cent headings.

NOTES

So far you have planned your speech as follows:

1. You have written it out in full.
2. You have extracted your key sentences.
3. You have polished your key sentences.
4. You have memorised your key sentences.
5. You have the feel of the whole speech, because you have repeated it several times.

Now you want to be certain that you won't forget anything during the speech.

Just a Scribble

Resting in one of his side pockets is a piece of paper on which are scribbled a few notes. When he made the notes he believed that they would be a help to him. He is on his feet, his speech has commenced, and he begins to slow down. He is err-ing and umm-ing—he is looking for his piece of paper—he has mislaid it— now he's drying up—ah, he's found it! He picks it up. He can't read it. He puts on his glasses . . . He gets going again. How that man is perspiring!

Many and many a time I have seen this happen. It can so easily be obviated. I have even seen men who are regular speakers using this scribble technique, and then wondering why they mumbled. A speaker always mumbles when he is trying to fathom out what his notes are about.

Never, never, never scribble notes on odd pieces of paper. You will either lose the paper, or you won't be able to read your notes.

Holding Papers

The chairman is finishing his introduction. We are all eager to hear the main speaker. The introduction is over, the speaker is standing up. We give him a warm smile of welcome—and then we notice what he has in his hand. A sheaf of papers. How many sheets? If only we could tell! He begins to speak. He lays down the papers while he goes on speaking for some time. He turns the first sheet over. He goes on again . . . then he turns over the next sheet. He picks up the sheaf of papers. That's better! Now we can see how much more there is to come. Good, it's the last sheet! No it isn't . . . There must have been three or four sheets stuck together. Now this is the last one—oh dear, it isn't! There's still another . . .

That's what happens when a speaker tries to hold a sheaf of papers in his hand while speaking. Also, if he isn't careful he will be waving them at his audience—and audiences don't like speakers to wave notes at them.

Don't hold notes in your hand if you can avoid doing so.

The Right Way

You must have notes, and you must know where to place them. If only speakers would give just a little thought before their speeches, not to the words they are going to say, but to their own comfort while speaking, their minds would be a lot easier.

Before you speak, decide where you are going to place your notes. Can you read them from that position? If not, you must do something about it. Before the dinner or meeting commences you must know where you are to be seated. When a speaker overlooks this elementary point he may find himself called upon to speak with his back to the table on which he has his notes.

Never be afraid of your notes. If you have not memorised your speech and you are going to use notes, don't try to hide them. Sir Winston Churchill never tries to hide his notes—he doesn't mind referring to them—it is all part of his speech. You can do the same. All that you have to be certain of is that you can read your notes easily.

CONFIDENCE CARDS

To be sure of taking all anxiety out of speech-making use Confidence Cards.

Think first of the alternatives:

A. Write all your sentences or headings on several sheets of paper. You can test for yourself the weakness of this system. Make up a speech and write it out. Now write all your leading sentences or headings on one or two sheets of paper. Stand up. Place the notes on a table. You will find that by the time you are half-way through your speech you will be peering, and nobody likes a peerer. You will be uncertain of your place. You can't bend down during a speech and tick off every point.

B. Divide a large sheet of paper into sections, and write the sentences or headings in separate squares on that one sheet. This sounds ideal, but in practice you will find it difficult to refer quickly to any particular square. There is nothing worse for a speaker than to look down and realise suddenly that he has a whole mass of notes and can't find his place.

C. Use large sheets of paper with your sentences or headings on each sheet. This can be effective, but it isn't always easy to prop up a large sheet of paper, or to find room for a large sheet of paper on a lectern or dining-table. Also, because you have so many sheets of paper, you will soon have your audience worrying as to the length of your speech.

The answer is to use cards. We call them Confidence Cards.

Why Cards?

Cards are so easy to handle. They are easy to separate. They can be carried in a side pocket. They don't become crumpled. They are easy to write upon. They can be held together by a ring, if necessary.

This is what you have to do:

1. Use as many cards as you have main steps or subsidiary steps in your speech.

2. Divide each card into three sections.

184 CONFIDENCE CARDS NEVER LET YOU DOWN

In the top left-hand section you will write your main sentence.

On the right-hand side you will have a space for exhibits.

Across the bottom you will have space for special points.

Right in the top corner of the right-hand section you will number each card.

They will look like this:

MAIN SENTENCE.	EXHIBITS.	No.
SPECIAL POINTS.		

In the left-hand section will be your main sentence for the step. Now assuming that you may want to use a visual aid during this step—a magnet, a chart, or a glass of water—this will be written in the section headed *exhibits*. If there is any point which you want to be absolutely sure of elaborating during the step, you can, under the third heading, make one or two further notes to which you may wish to refer. Or you can write a subsidiary sentence.

And so you will continue, card after card for each step—your main sentences, exhibits, special points, subsidiary sentences.

Even if the cards have to be held in your hand, they don't look nearly so bad as a sheaf of papers. Small cards can be almost invisible if held in the palm of the hand and, if linked together, they won't fall.

They are easy to read, so easy to turn over, so easy to refer to if you want to read a fact, so easy to put away when the speech is over . . .

Using the Cards

Write on one side of the cards only, and write or print legibly. Before the speech commences, place your cards in front of you so that you can read them easily.

Often you will find that you will make your whole speech without having to refer to the cards at all, but having them in front of you will give you great confidence.

This is how you might prepare a card for one of the main steps in a speech on *Magic and Sleight of Hand* :

"A conjurer thinks of something impossible, something against natural laws—then he tries to do it. You could not imagine a man swallowing first a packet of needles, then a reel of thread, chewing hard and then slowly drawing the thread from his mouth with all the needles threaded on it, could you? Yet Harry Houdini, greatest of all magicians, did that very thing. But conjurers are never satisfied, and as soon as they see a good trick they start to think how they can improve it. In consequence, the next step was to use something even more deadly looking than needles, and Will Goldston decided on razor blades. When doing the trick this way, the magician first takes out a razor blade and cuts a piece of paper with it—like this! Then the sequence is as before, first swallow several blades, then the thread, and as with the needles draw the thread slowly from the mouth with the blades threaded on it."

This is how it would look on a Confidence Card:

Main Sentence.	Exhibit.	3
A CONJURER THINKS OF SOMETHING IMPOSSIBLE, SOMETHING AGAINST NATURAL LAWS—THEN HE TRIES TO DO IT.	RAZOR BLADE. PAPER.	
SPECIAL POINTS. Names: HARRY HOUDINI. WILL GOLDSTON.		

Look at that card again. If you had to use the part of the speech which I have quoted above, you could do it readily with these few words on the card. As soon as you had said:

"A conjurer thinks of something impossible,

> something against natural laws—then he tries to
> do it . . ."

and had taken in at a glance the names Houdini and
Goldston, you could speak for several minutes until
you were ready for the next step. Then one more glance
at the next card, if necessary, and you would be well
away once more.

PRACTISE

Practise with these cards. Rehearse with them time
and time again. As soon as you have got used to hand-
ling them you will never think of making a speech
without them. The cards should be approximately the
size of a post card, but they may be smaller. I use cards
5 ins. by 3 ins.

To give you practice, refer back to your speech on
the *Welfare State*. You should have polished up those
sentences. Now enter the sentences on cards; add some
subsidiary points. You will amaze yourself by being
able to deliver the speech perfectly, just by referring
to these brief sentences.

To help you make out your Confidence Cards after
reading through your speech on the Welfare State,
I am showing you how I prepared a speech on '*Sales
Managers*'. The speech followed an invitation by a
body of sales executives, asking me to speak strongly
on the subject, as markets were hardening and some
sales managers did not appear to be adapting themselves to the changing conditions. The sentences *in
italics* are those which I transferred to the Confidence
Cards.

Speech on Sales Managers

**Step 1.
Story Opening**

No man is a hero to his own wife, and that is why I bought a dog. There had been burglars in the road, and my wife had the unkind idea that I might send her down first if there were noises in the night. So I bought a dog—or rather, I was sold a small bundle of fur by a good dog salesman. He assured me that it would awaken the whole neighbourhood at the slightest sound. It didn't even awaken itself when the window was broken, and we found the poor dog unconscious and the silver gone. I went back to the dog salesman to complain.

"Ah," he answered, "what you need now is a bigger dog to look after the little dog."

**Step 2.
Interest**

Managing directors have been engaging bigger and better dogs for some time. I am referring to the stream of actuaries, merchandising men, accountants and statisticians who now watch over the sales manager. That this has been brought about is largely his own fault. Because sales managers had little to do during the period of the sellers' market they bombarded their directors with reports, maps, compilations of their research activities, and so on. But they forgot their men. They overlooked the fact that the most important side of sales management is the human side.

**Quotation
and Anecdote**

Henry Ford once said that he would rather employ a sales manager who understood men and could get the best out of them, than a sales manager with actuarial knowledge, who presented him daily with bigger and better charts, and more and more figures. The only figures a director wants from his sales manager are rising sales figures. Naturally, he also wants to keep his sales costs low, but the most inexpensive sales aid a sales manager possesses is his ability to get loyal men to work hard for him.

Analogy

This he can only achieve if he understands human relations. A sales manager without an understanding of human relations is like a doctor with no love for his vocation. Neither salesman nor patient will have much regard for such a man.

Step 3.
Confidence

In twenty-five years' experience of marketing, I have never yet met a salesman who did not react to justifiable praise. But how many sales managers do praise their salesmen? Yet that is a fundamental of human relations. Many are quick to dictate letters of reprimand when salesmen really need encouragement. If a man has been working conscientiously, what good will it do to write to him to complain that his results are poor, and to insist upon him working harder? It is a sales manager's job to find out why the salesman's figures are dropping, and then to help him to increase his sales.

Main Step 4

Too many sales managers to-day have worked their way up from the top. There is no substitute for road experience. Men without this experience should pick up a bag and go right out and sell. They will then learn for themselves what it feels like to telephone head office after a blank day. The telephone to some executives is an instrument of dictatorship. You can tell it by the way they pick it up. It's a snatch. Their voices alter. They no longer speak in well-modulated tones—they bark. A salesman? What a nuisance!

Anecdote Henry Burn is an example of the ideal sales manager. Have any of you ever telephoned him? If you have, you will know that I am speaking the truth. He always seems so pleased to hear from you. I have been in his office when a salesman has 'phoned. Harry's voice is quiet and friendly, and the salesman is made to feel that his sales manager is delighted to speak to him. When the conversation is over the salesman has benefited from the talk, and will sell all the better for it. Can *we* say that of *our* telephone conversations with our men? And now from telephones to buzzers.

Main Step 5 *Do you like pressing buzzers?* I did when I first became a sales manager. I also liked my comfortable office chair. I appreciated it so much that I never wanted to leave it. Letter writing—yes. Bulletin writing—yes. Pep talks—yes. Trunk calls—yes . . .

Quotation One day I found a card on my desk. On it was written this quotation: "True friends visit us in prosperity by invitation, but in adversity they come without being asked." It had been placed there by my managing director. One of my salesmen had been ill. Another had not been doing so well. There had been a few complaints from customers . . . I took the hint, picked up my bag, and went out visiting and selling.

Main Step 6. Dr. Johnson said, "*To be happy at home*
Quotation *is the ultimate result of all ambition.*" When
Evidence a sales manager visits a salesman and takes an interest in his family, he is

helping to create that happiness in the home which is so essential to the salesman. But not only should we visit our salesmen and our customers. We should also call upon prospective customers. What a fine example we set when at a meeting of salesmen we can tell them that we intend to break new ground for them. A sales manager doing that? Almost unheard of! But it's the kind of thing which builds up a loyal team of salesmen.

Anecdote Many of you know Charles Wayne, he is certainly one of the most able executives in this country. He makes a point of going out to sell three or four times a year. He told me that when he first became sales manager he asked to be allowed to spend the major part of his time selling with each of his men. Only when he had done that did he devote his energies to direction from the office. If he, one of the busiest of executives, can do that, then all of us can.

Main Step 7 *Have you ever kept a good man down?* Knowing many of you so well makes the question seem pointless, but it is a fact that some sales managers keep their best salesmen down, because they are afraid of their own jobs. That is wrong. If ever we are afraid of losing our position, we shall lose it all right. The best way for a sales manager to safeguard his position and even achieve further promotion, perhaps to board level, is to build up men to take his place.

Anecdote One of the most brilliant leaders of industry, Duke, head of the first of the tobacco combines, was once asked for a recipe for success. He answered:

Quotation "There are three essentials, the first is men; the second is men; and the third is men." We must all remember that. We cannot hope to maintain success unless we have around us first-class men. It is our job, therefore, to be man-builders. When we find good men, we must try to understand them, to guide them, to direct them if necessary, to appreciate them, and always to help them.

Main Step 8. (Read from newspaper) *Husband leaves Hollywood beauty queen and runs away with cook.* (*pause*) Obviously, man cannot live on love alone, but then neither can a salesman live on understanding and friendship alone. He must have a good income as well. The successful sales manager not only believes in human relations, but he knows that his sales force must be well rewarded for the work they do. Now this is dangerous ground, but you have asked me to give my opinion on the subject of incentives, and here it is : I believe that all salesmen should be rewarded by incentives, but I don't think that an annual bonus is a good enough incentive. Salesmen should receive a basic salary and commission on all sales made. The more they sell, the more they should earn. When I raise this point with executives who pay fixed salaries with some small bonus scheme attached, they usually tell me that they will consider incentives on a larger scale when trade becomes difficult. Alternatively, they tell me that their salesmen prefer fixed salaries.

Anecdote A friend of mine once had a perfect secretary. For all that, she was slightly underpaid. However, to show his appreciation of her work he told her that he would pay for her to have a holiday abroad. On board ship she met a stock-broker and his wife. They became friendly, and on her return he offered her a job at fifty per cent more salary than she was getting. My friend told me that that taught him a lesson. Now he knows that there is no substitute for people receiving a reward commensurate with their efforts. Holidays, bonus schemes, vouchers, prizes—these don't take the place of commission. He learned another lesson, too. Now he pays his staff what he would pay to replace any members if they left him. If we lose a good sales-man because he is not earning enough money with us, how much will his replacement cost us? If a sales-man is reaping a just reward for his efforts, then he doesn't want to leave his job.

Statistics The next point is that the men are supposed to prefer fixed salaries. I can only answer that we asked 162 salesmen who were being paid fixed salaries (some, it is true, had small bonuses as well) if they would prefer to carry on on their present terms, or would rather change to a lower salary, plus a commission. 159 of them told us that they would be much happier if they were given an opportunity of earning a higher income through increased sales. A knowledge of human relations teaches us human weaknesses. Men should work as hard as they can, no matter how they are rewarded —but they don't.

You may well answer that you can drive them to reach their quotas.

Main Step 9 *Dynamic drive is breaking out all over him.* I heard that expression the other day. It was used in connection with a sales manager whose managing director had told him that he must achieve better results. He decided to drive his salesmen. But it is useless for a sales manager to keep drumming into his men that they must work harder, and to keep hurling threats at them if they do not succeed. It is of little use stepping up their quotas, sending them telegrams, giving them pep talks . . . If that is drive, do we want any part of it? The real drive which helps to increase sales is the drive put out from the sales manager's office. The new ideas he produces, the new sales aids he designs, special features about the products, sales competitions, and most of all, the sight of him in the field are the real incentives the men require to increase their efforts. Perhaps, then, drive is not such a bad word—if we remember that it is up to the sales manager to drive himself to success.

Main Step 10.
Summary
Close

The successful sales manager, then, appreciates his men, praises them often and criticises them rarely. He is pleased to hear from them and takes an interest in their families. He meets them regularly and sells with them regularly. He fights hard to see that they get a good reward for their efforts. He drives himself for their benefit. In other words, he is a *go-giver*.

And here is how I made out the Confidence Cards:

	1
NO MAN IS A HERO TO HIS OWN WIFE AND THAT IS WHY I BOUGHT A DOG.	

DOG SALESMAN
STORY.

	2
MANAGING DIRECTORS HAVE BEEN ENGAGING BIGGER AND BETTER DOGS.	

ACCOUNTANTS, etc.
HENRY FORD STORY (FIGURES).
HUMAN RELATIONS ANALOGY.

	3
IN TWENTY-FIVE YEARS' EXPERIENCE OF MARKETING.	

VALUE OF PRAISE.
HELP SALESMEN, DON'T
CRITICISE.

TOO MANY SALES MANAGERS TO-DAY HAVE WORKED THEIR WAY UP FROM THE TOP.

PICK UP A SALES-MAN'S KIT.

4

TELEPHONE.
HENRY BURN STORY.

DO YOU LIKE PRESSING BUZZERS?

5

ME—ARMCHAIR SALES MANAGER.
QUOTE—TRUE FRIENDS VISIT US IN PROSPERITY BY INVITATION, BUT IN ADVERSITY THEY COME WITHOUT BEING ASKED.

DR. JOHNSON SAID, "TO BE HAPPY AT HOME IS THE ULTIMATE RESULT OF ALL AMBITION."

6

VISITING SALESMEN.
CHARLES WAYNE STORY.

HAVE YOU EVER KEPT A GOOD MAN DOWN?	7

DUKE.

THREE ESSENTIALS FOR SUCCESS.
MEN—MEN—MEN.
BUILD MEN.

HUSBAND LEAVES HOLLYWOOD BEAUTY QUEEN AND RUNS AWAY WITH COOK.	8
	NEWSPAPER.

INCENTIVES.
SECRETARY STORY.
162 SALESMEN—159 *FOR*.

DYNAMIC DRIVE IS BREAKING OUT ALL OVER HIM.	9

WHAT IS DRIVE?

PEP TALKS ⎫
TELEGRAMS ⎬ NO.
QUOTAS ⎭

THE SUCCESSFUL SALES MANA-
GER, THEN, APPRECIATES HIS
MEN, PRAISES THEM OFTEN,
AND CRITICISES RARELY.

10

GO-GIVER.

CHAPTER XV

Making Them Laugh

"Corn," said the comedian, "corn—why, they love it!"

We were at the King's Head Hotel, Sheffield. Some of the artists appearing at the local theatre had joined us, and a merry time was being had by all. After a while one member of the party became a little awkward, tending to spoil the general merriment by accusing those who try to make us laugh of rarely changing their acts. Things were becoming a little heated, when the 'top-of-the-bill' comic gave his dissertation on 'corn'.

"If," he said, "you give the public anything new, they don't like it. They prefer the same old thing over and over again; corn—why, they love it!"

My brother and I did not take sides in this discussion, but later we talked about it. We came to the conclusion—perhaps wrongly—that audiences may love corn in the shape of old melodies, but they do not appreciate hearing the same stories week after week. If only they wouldn't laugh quite so heartily out of sympathy for the comedians, I am sure these artists would improve their scripts.

Corn is well to the fore in public speaking. It is rare, indeed, for a speaker to talk for any length of time without telling two or three jokes. Lecturers on even the dullest subjects manage to find room to tell a story; possibly they like to think of themselves as men of dry humour, but so often it is old gags that they repeat.

Do remember that it isn't essential for a speaker to tell funny stories, although if a story is a good one and well told it can help the speech along.

Find the Stories

Joke books don't help the public speaker a great deal, unless he is prepared to use his imagination in conjunction with any story he borrows from them. You must never repeat any story that you have read, word for word. The best way for a speaker to build up his stock of stories is to keep a notebook and record them as he hears them. You will find many of the best stories printed in magazines and publications such as *The Reader's Digest*.

If you haven't a fund of stories, and your notebook is not yet completed, then you may have to refer to joke books. In this event, if you alter the stories to suit yourself, all will be well. Often you can find several ideas in the same story. For example, here is a story which was printed in a magazine:

> *We know a gentleman who, after a medical examination, was told by the doctor that he was in pretty bad shape. "Too little blood in your alcohol stream."*

As an exercise for our students we asked them to think around this story, evolve another from it and include it in a speech. It was told in at least eight different ways. Here are two of them:

> "A friend of mine is a salesman for a wine and spirit merchant. He samples his wares with all the customers, and in between times too—

just to keep him in form. Do you know what the Inland Revenue authorities did? They charged back to him the benefits received! But that was nothing! He happens to be a blood donor, and they charged the recipients of his blood with benefits as well."

Another told it in this way:

"When I was in the army I had to have a blood transfusion. They checked up on me, but they couldn't find my group. They sent for another doctor and he checked up on me. In the end he turned to the nurse and said, 'Take away that plasma. Just put up a bottle of Scotch!'"

Most stories can be adapted to line up with your speech.

Two Warnings

Here is a warning for all speakers: Don't be too worried if you tell your story and you don't raise a laugh. I include four stories in one of my lectures which are generally appreciated. On several occasions, however, one or two of them have misfired. Why they should go down well on some occasions and not on others, I don't know. Don't think you have failed in your story-telling because your story falls flat, but check up on it just the same.

The next warning is: Don't tell stories about your children. There are many good stories about youngsters which you can alter to suit yourself, but true stories about our own families never seem to go down well. Perhaps it is the family environment that is missing, or perhaps the human touch. Family stories are rarely funny to those outside the family circle.

Introducing the Story

Never warn an audience that you are about to tell them a story. Too many speakers use these introductions:

> "I heard a good one the other day . . ."
> "This story rather bears out what I was saying . . ."
> "Have you heard this one . . ."
> "One of the funniest stories I have heard on this subject is . . ."

There is one exception to this rule, and that applies to the lecturer who rarely tells a humorous story. If he is lecturing to students, they may be a little frightened of him, and because of this they are liable to let the story pass without a smile—only to realise a few sentences further on that the lecturer was, in fact, trying to be funny.

If you have to lecture on a serious subject and you intend to introduce a humorous story, then you may have to give warning of its approach or, alternatively, change your expression, and smile as you begin to tell the story. Then the audience will smile with you.

Dialect

Not many speakers can tell a good story in dialect. There are only two alternatives to adopt if you decide to tell a story like this. You can practise the dialect for days before the speech, to make sure that you are able to tell it properly. Or you need not use the dialect.

More often than not, a story sounds just as effective when told in your own straightforward manner.

Take Care

Do your best to avoid stories with a racial or a religious background. Otherwise you may offend some members of your audience.

Bring In the Audience

At many functions a cabaret takes place after dinner. It is a standard practice of comedians on these occasions to ask members of the organising committee for the names of some of the people present, to enable them to bring these names into their stories.

This technique can be used by a speaker. However, he must be careful not to embarrass anyone. If he takes care in this respect, he is bound to win applause.

Use Newspapers

A speaker can often make good use of a newspaper during a speech.

One speaker, giving a talk on our export trade, used the newspaper story technique in this way: He picked it up, opened it carefully, and said,

> "Did you see this morning's *Express*? What fine headlines—full employment! Never have there been so many people employed in this country . . ."

He read on for a few lines, and then, laying the paper down, he said,

> "Did you know that some of our civil servants are so worried about their jobs that the labour

exchanges are employing touts to pull in a few people to make them take unemployment benefits?"

He got his laugh, and using the newspaper for demonstration helped to break up his speech.

Slow It Down

I don't tell stories particularly well, that is why I rarely tell them in conversation. At one time I would never tell a story in a speech. For some unknown reason, as soon as I had to tell a story I would start gabbling. I suppose it was some deep fear that I would forget the end, and therefore I wanted to get it over quickly.

It doesn't worry me any more, because I have found the answer.

The answer is to slow down the whole story. Slow it down with pauses—even a couple of err's and umm's won't hurt. When you get to the punch line, make certain that it is spoken slowly and distinctly.

If you don't do this you will find that many members of the audience won't laugh, because they won't have understood your story. Others will turn to their neighbours, obviously whispering, "What did he say?" or "What was the end?"

You don't want that to happen. Slow the story down, and particularly slow down at the end.

Laughing

You have probably been told a story by the 'laughing' funny man.

He starts laughing at his own story within a few

seconds of commencing to tell it, and from there on it is punctuated with his own hearty laughs.

It is true that laughter may be contagious, but not under those circumstances.

Don't laugh at your own jokes while you are telling them. Many teachers object to a speaker laughing when he has finished his story, but I don't think there is anything wrong in that. If he enjoys the telling of it as much as his audience enjoys listening to it, then there is no harm in his chuckling as he finishes the punch line—or smiling, anyway.

Rehearse Your Stories

I have known speakers to rehearse their speeches over and over again, but many of them don't trouble to rehearse their stories—they are quite sure that everyone will enjoy them.

If you have two or three good stories to tell, do try them out on someone before the speech. Try them on your friends or your family. If the reaction is bad, don't blame them for their lack of humour—scrap the story.

A Must

The one 'must' for all humorous stories is: The story must line up with the speech.

Don't drag in a story just because it is a good one. I know it is a big temptation to do this, and I have done it over and over again—but I don't do it any longer. It doesn't pay.

What happens is this: You have your speech all worked out. Then a friend tells you a story which you consider really funny, and you feel that you must introduce it into your speech. You do so. Suddenly you switch from the subject matter of the speech into your new story. The audience is bewildered, cannot see the point of it, and it falls flat.

Keep away from that kind of story.

Act the Part

Even if you cannot use a dialect, you can still act a part. Act all of the parts when telling a story. If a child is introduced into the story, then sound a little child-like. If a sergeant-major participates, then make yourself sound like a sergeant-major. A public speaker must, on occasion, be part actor, to make his story more amusing.

Keep it Clean

Keep to clean stories. They can be just as funny as the other kind.

Stories in bad taste may appeal to some members of a stag party, but usually they are embarrassing. The most embarrassing example I have ever heard was at an association dinner. Towards the end of his speech, the speaker said,

"There are only two or three ladies here, but would they mind leaving the room now . . ."

He said this with a smirk. The women left the room, and he then proceeded to tell a story which could not have appealed even to the dregs of humanity.

That is an extreme case, but too many speakers think they can raise a laugh by telling a story with a double meaning.

Commander Campbell, who achieved fame in the

first of the Brains Trusts, told me that in no circumstances would he tell a story which could not be listened to by every member of a family. He is, of course, renowned for his stories—he is one of our best raconteurs.

He told me that once after a dinner at which there were ladies present, the port was passed round after the ladies left the room. He had already made his speech, but the chairman then said, "Now that the women have gone you can tell us some of your real stories." Campbell said that he then told a few ultra-clean stories. When he had finished he said, "I never tell any of the other kind, whether there are ladies present or not."

He feels as strongly about it as that—and that's how I feel about it, too.

ALL GOOD FUN

There are various kinds of humorous stories, and ways of bringing humour into a speech.

The Anecdote
The anecdote is easily the best of all humorous stories. Tell a story, apparently true, introduce yourself into that story, and you have the best way of raising a laugh.

The Humorous Story
This is the standard funny yarn that goes the rounds. Everyone knows it is a stock story, but provided it is a good one, it can always be introduced.

The Subtle Story

The subtle story must be handled with care—you cannot rely on it being understood by the audience. If they do not, they may still be puzzling it all out while you are in a most impassioned part of your speech.

The stage comedian who tells a subtle story can deliberately pause at the end of it, make some remark about it, and wait for the applause; if he feels that there is anyone who hasn't understood it he can even explain it for their benefit. A speaker cannot do that. He has to get on with his speech.

The Wisecrack

Here is a favourite with our friends from across the sea. Often American speakers introduce quite a few wisecracks.

There is no reason why they should not be used except that they may be too quickfire for the audience.

I once heard Bob Hope say that he was quite satisfied if the audience got one in three of his cracks. That's all right for Bob Hope. He and his script writers are so brilliant that he can follow one story with another, one quip with another, and they are all so good that if one of them is missed the next one hits home. The speaker may only have one wisecrack to use, and if that isn't understood, then it is wasted.

If you use a wisecrack, do make sure that you speak slowly.

The Epigram

This does not come under the heading of a humorous story, but, if used effectively, it can raise as good a laugh as any story. Sir Winston Churchill is a master of the epigram. In one second he can move us to tears, and a second afterwards a brilliant sentence will change our mood to laughter.

The Pun

Here the advice is simple—never use a pun.

The Humorous Poem

Yes, you may be able to introduce a short humorous poem or jingle, but it must be a short one. If it is more than a few lines, don't bother about it.

The Sarcastic Story

It is sometimes possible to get a laugh by being sarcastic. Don't do it.

The Leg-Pull

Often, gentle and kindly leg-pulling can raise a laugh.

If it is at the expense of some of your good friends who are sitting at the table with you, and who will enjoy the leg-pulling as much as the audience, then there is no harm in indulging in it. Good-natured fun doesn't hurt anyone. Best of all, however, is to make fun of yourself.

There is a lot of fun in speaking in public, and a great deal of entertainment can be derived by a speaker from being able to tell a really humorous story.

Keep to the rules, and all will be well.

CHAPTER XVI

Hecklers and Question Time

THE story is told of Charles Lamb that on one occasion he was giving a talk when someone in the crowd interrupted him continuously by hissing. Finally, Lamb could stand it no longer, and said in a quiet voice: *There are only three things that hiss, a goose, a snake and a fool. Will you come up on to the platform and be identified?*

That may or may not be a true story, but it is not always easy for a speaker to find just the right answer which will win applause from the audience, and will silence the heckler. Heckling doesn't do much harm, and it rarely happens to speakers, anyway.

Some speakers bring their own hecklers with them. The following 'heckle' and answer is one that I must have heard a half-dozen times:

The heckler continuously cries out, "Liar!"

After a while the speaker pauses, and then pointing at the heckler says,

> "If the gentleman who keeps interrupting would not mind telling us his name, instead of merely shouting his calling, we should all be pleased to meet him."

It always gets a laugh.

Oscar Wilde, a master of repartee, was believed to have thought out all his brilliant answers many months before he used them. He would, when the occasion arose, try so to develop a conversation that he would be able to show his scintillating wit.

If you think that you may be heckled, work on the same lines. You will have a shrewd idea of what a heckler is likely to call out, and you can prepare your answers in advance.

If you are heckled during a speech, there are three things you can do:

> You can ignore it.
> You can be polite about it.
> You can lose your temper.

Ignore a heckler as much as you can. That is the best advice. Either he will get tired of his heckling, or he will be quietened by members of the audience sitting near to him.

You can try to get the better of him in a polite manner or by the quickness of your wit, but you must never lose your temper with him.

As soon as a speaker loses his temper with a heckler, the audience is tempted to take sides against the speaker.

QUESTION TIME

The success of question time depends so much upon your chairman. If he is strong, and only allows those questions which come within the scope of your speech, the session can be enjoyed by all—including the speaker. If he is a weak chairman, then the speaker may find himself in difficulties with some of the questions raised.

Here are some of the ways a speaker can tackle difficult questions:

Agreeing

Disarm the questioner, and relax the audience, by using this *agreement technique*: If you answer a question too quickly it will look as though you have rehearsed the whole thing, that you knew what was going to be asked, and you have your answer ready.

This may well be the fact, but you don't want to let the audience know just how clever you are. They prefer a speaker who isn't too clever.

Listen to the question carefully. The chairman should repeat it. Pause for a second and then say, "I agree, there is a lot in what you say, but . . ."

This technique tends to calm down an irritated questioner and makes him feel that he is a sensible fellow and that you agree with much of what he has had to say.

The Turnabout Answer

Here is an example of a *turnabout answer*.

QUESTION: "But if you build the road in that direction it will spoil the amenities."

SPEAKER: "Let me put it to you in this way: If you don't build the road there you won't have any amenities to spoil."

By turning the question round the speaker helps to show the weaknesses of the questioner's argument.

Why?

No speaker wishes to become involved in an argument with a questioner, but sometimes it is a good thing to allow a questioner to elaborate his remarks. To do this, the speaker simply uses the one word—

Why?

For example:

QUESTION: "The housing list is completely unfair."

SPEAKER: "Why?"

QUESTIONER: "Because newcomers to the district seem to have precedence over some of those who have lived here for years."

SPEAKER: "Why?"

QUESTIONER: "I don't know why."

SPEAKER: "That is the point. If you did know why you would not have raised the question. The answer is . . ."

The word *why* can be of considerable help to a speaker during question-time.

The Foolish Question

Often a foolish question is raised—one which can so easily lead to an argument because it is so senseless.

The best thing that a speaker can do, in the circumstances, is to laugh it off and ask for another question.

Insults

If the speaker is insulted he has two alternatives. He can ignore the insult, or he can answer it.

Sometimes it is best to ignore it. On other occasions it is better to adopt this attitude: Stop speaking and try to get some quietness in the room. Then ask the questioner to repeat his question.

A person often quite willing to shout his insults in a

tumult, may not be so ready to voice his opinions when all is quiet. Usually, he will look embarrassed and say nothing. If he should repeat the insult, then the speaker can only appeal to the chair for order.

Be Stumped

Don't be too clever. You need not answer all questions off pat. If a question is of small importance, it matters little if it stumps you, or apparently stumps you.

"I'm afraid I cannot answer that one," said with a laugh, can win over quite a few people in the audience to your side.

WELCOME THEM

Question-time is a good testing time for the speaker. He should welcome questions. He should not be irritated by having to clarify some point which he feels should be clear to the most unintelligent members of the audience. The more questions he has to answer, the better must have been his speech. It means that the speaker has really interested his audience.

Show as much interest in answering the questions as you did in making the speech, and you will finish the evening in good style.

CHAPTER XVII

When You are the Chairman

THE subject was a simple one for the speaker. He was a well-known writer of fast-moving detective stories, and he was to give a talk on *How To Write A Thriller*.

The chairman introducing him had not been speaking for long before the author began to look harassed. Most of the facts that the chairman had given about the speaker's literary reputation were incorrect. He told us that he did not enjoy detective stories. Then he proceeded to relate a series of anecdotes connected with Scotland Yard. Finally, he gave his version of how he thought a detective story should be written.

The poor speaker! We all felt so sorry for him, but not nearly so sorry as he must have been feeling for himself.

Not many chairmen are as bad as this; nevertheless, the standard of chairmanship can, undoubtedly, be improved.

Choosing the Chairman

Until the time arrives—and I don't suppose it ever will—when chairmen are chosen because they are good chairmen, and not just because they are people of some importance, speakers will always have chairman troubles. Too often they are chosen because of their wealth, because they are popular men, or because someone wants to flatter them.

They should be chosen for their qualities as

chairmen, in the same way as speakers are invited to speak because of their qualities as speakers.

It is the duty of men or women who, because of their good work, may be elected to become chairmen and will, therefore, be presiding at many meetings, to study not only the standard duties of a chairman, but also the relationship between a chairman and a visiting speaker.

TYPES OF CHAIRMEN

Does it apply to me is with us again. Read how some chairmen act, and then ask yourself if you are guilty of some of their mistakes:

The Lackadaisical Chairman

He does not take the trouble to get his facts correct. Knowing little about a speaker, he makes something up and hopes that his ambiguous remarks will be near enough true.

The reason many a speaker has to create confidence in himself at the beginning of a speech is because this type of chairman does not create audience confidence for him.

It is the duty of a chairman to find out something about the speaker's background, and briefly to acquaint the audience with the qualities of the man or woman they are about to hear.

The Flatterer

He tries to make up for his lack of knowledge of a speaker by highly-coloured flattering remarks. This only undermines the confidence of a speaker, who

knows that he cannot possibly live up to these blandish-
ments.

The Director

This type of chairman is a demanding chairman. He
wants to tell the speaker in advance just what is
expected of him. He directs the speaker, as a judge
directs a jury. He is not concerned with what the
speaker has planned. He insists upon answers to the
questions he has in mind. He uses remarks such as
these :

> "No doubt he will tell us . . ."
> "We are all eagerly awaiting his thoughts
> upon . . ."
> "He will, of course, answer these questions which
> we have in our minds . . ."
> "He is sure to inform us . . ."

This can be most disturbing to a speaker who has
not planned his speech on the lines indicated by the
chairman.

The Thief

How proud he is of his research work! This chairman does take trouble about the subject—but in the
wrong direction.

He investigates, he thinks, he asks questions. Then,
on the night of the speech, he airs his knowledge. He
steals the speaker's thunder. Finally, he sits down with
a self-satisfied look, while the poor speaker stands up
wondering what he is going to talk about.

The Great-I-am

A most important man! He is doing everyone a favour by acting as chairman. He is not interested in what it is all about. He rushes in at the last moment, and even while shaking hands with the speaker he is talking to someone else.

I heard one such chairman who arrived only five minutes before a meeting ask, "Who is this fellow? What has he done?"

How wrong! How unkind!

The Humorist

He has a string of stories to tell, and he is going to tell them, however long he keeps the speaker waiting. Another thief, this man—he wants to steal the limelight!

Chairman/Speaker

He is easy to define: He doesn't so much introduce the speaker—he makes the speech himself.

The Weak Chairman

He lets everything get out of hand. He is scared of upsetting the speaker, scared of upsetting the audience, frightened of saying the wrong thing, frightened of keeping to a time-table, frightened to stop the over-offensive questioner and, in consequence, ruins our evening for us.

The Seeker

He is always seeking information. While he is on the platform, just prior to the speaker commencing his speech, he will beckon to someone. He will ask them questions, and he will repeat this act. Then he will talk to the secretary.

This delays the meeting, and it doesn't help the speaker at all.

Even during the speech this chairman will keep on beckoning and muttering asides. All most disturbing and showing a complete lack of organising ability.

THE IDEAL CHAIRMAN

He is firm and friendly. He has thought things out in advance. He has his facts right, and presents them briefly. He doesn't try to steal the limelight—in fact he would rather move off the platform and so leave it to the speaker. He knows the rules and he keeps to them.

HE REALISES THAT HE IS A HOST, and he means to be a good one.

IN THE CHAIR

Here are some of the rules which the *ideal chairman* remembers:

The Chairman's Personality

You have to alter your manner to suit the occasion. If you are introducing someone who is going to make a light-hearted speech, then your style should not be the same as when you are introducing a professor of economics.

Help the Speaker

Do put the speaker into the picture. Tell him how long your opening address will last; tell him how you are going to conclude so that he will know, a few seconds before you have finished, that it will soon be his turn to stand up.

If you don't do this, you will have the speaker looking anxiously at you, wondering when you are going to stop. I have seen many a speaker half rise in his chair as he thought the chairman was finishing, only to have to sit back as the chairman continued with his introduction.

Courtesy

I have heard speakers introduced by chairmen in glowing terms. The audience has felt that here was a speaker whom the chairman looked upon not only as a great authority, but as a personal friend.

Then the speech ends. The chairman mutters a few words, and darts off the platform.

The chairman should always thank the speaker in a proper manner at the conclusion of a speech.

And here is discourtesy of a different kind:

Important members of an association greet a speaker with enthusiasm, he is announced by the chairman, the speech is made and well applauded. The chairman then disappears to meet his cronies, and the speaker is ignored. I have often seen a speaker who, half an hour previously, has been wildly acclaimed by members of an organisation, sitting on his own in a corner of the room, looking thoroughly disappointed at the fact that nobody has taken the trouble to look after him.

It is the chairman's job to look after the speaker, not only before he speaks, but also to see that hospitality is extended for the rest of the evening. That is common courtesy.

The chairman should arrange to meet the speaker some time before the meeting starts and help him all he can. After the speech the speaker should be invited to join the chairman's party.

Time and Order

The chairman must make quite sure that a speaker (or, if there are several speakers, that each one of them) knows exactly how long he is expected to speak.

If there are several speakers on the platform, do let them know in advance where they are to be seated.

Look Interested

The speech has commenced. What happens? Many a chairman feels that his work is done, and he can now concentrate on other things. He wipes his forehead; he blows his nose; he smiles at various members of the audience; makes a comment to a neighbour; fidgets— in fact, does everything to spoil the speaker's speech.

The good chairman should, for the most part of the talk, look as if he were absorbed in what is being said.

Humour

What I have written on this subject for speakers applies also to chairmen. It is not necessary for a chairman to tell a funny story, although many seem to think it is. If you do tell one, be certain that it links up with the main speech—and also, be certain it is a short story.

A Break

The good chairman plans in advance the breaks which may have to take place during a long series of speeches.

It is very difficult for an audience to sit still for several hours while five or six people speak. It is far better for the chairman to announce after two speeches that there will be a short break.

FOUR DUTIES OF A CHAIRMAN

1. He must maintain order and see that there is respect for the chair. Should there be a question-time, he must make certain that the questions asked are relevant; otherwise he must not allow them.
2. He must prevent questioners from making speeches.
3. He must not allow any offensive expressions.
4. He must be impartial.

COMMITTEE MEETINGS

If you are acting as chairman for a committee or general meeting, you will usually find that the secretary will provide you with all the information you require. Do, however, become acquainted with any rules which may apply, and don't forget that if you are part of a group of people who wish to elect you as chairman, that group must first of all appoint an acting chairman, who will then ask for nominations for the official chairman. Only when you are elected will you preside.

Minutes

The secretary will first read the minutes of the previous meeting. If it is agreed that they are a correct version of the business transacted, then you will sign the record. If any discrepancy comes to light, then you have the power, if it is agreed that a mistake has been made, to alter the minute, and you must initial the alteration.

Agenda

Keep to the agenda. Do not allow any motion to be brought forward which is not on the agenda.

A Motion

A motion is merely a formal proposal; it must be a positive declaration. When the motion has been read to the meeting, no debate can take place on it until it has been seconded. Only after the proposer of the motion and the seconder have spoken, can there be any supporting speeches.

When the debate has finished you will put the question to the vote.

After the motion has been put forward and seconded, a member of the committee can put forward an amendment. The amendment must not be negative to the resolution; if it were a direct negative, it would be something which obviously would take place in the main vote on the motion. The amendment can only be to add something to the motion, or to take something away. The amendment is put to the vote after it has been seconded, and if it is not carried, the original motion stands.

There are, of course, many rules applying to motions and amendments, but they need not worry the average speaker who becomes a chairman.

For those entering politics it is a different matter.

They will have to acquaint themselves with all procedures referring to motions, amendments and debates.

The Casting Vote

Many chairmen believe that they have a casting vote. That is not always the case, and the chairman should look up *standing orders* before taking the chair, to make certain whether, in fact, he does have a casting vote.

DEBATE

Debates are nearly always interesting, provided the chairman knows his job. A debate can become a useless harangue, and a complete waste of time, if it is governed by a weak chairman.

Before the debate commences, the chairman should tell the audience what they are going to have to decide. The points at issue at debates are often so involved that no-one knows what they are voting for when it is all over. While a speaker is expounding his views, listen attentively. Should he talk on matters outside the scope of the debate you must interrupt to ask him to keep to his brief.

A chairman is also entitled to ask a speaker who has gone over his allotted time to close his speech.

When the debate is over, the chairman will, very briefly, state the points at issue again, and then put them to the vote.

At the conclusion of a debate, and after the vote has been taken, the chairman will say a few words of praise to the loser and also congratulate the winner.

DISCUSSION GROUPS

Discussion groups formed to discuss points raised by a speaker must also have a chairman. If ever a strong chairman were needed, it is surely under these conditions, because someone is bound to try to monopolise the discussions. It is up to the chairman to stop this kind of thing. When a member of the group has made a point, the chairman should not allow him to continue. He must give each member a chance to express his views.

When the chairman feels that the subject has been fully discussed, and that all opinions have been expressed, then he should stop the discussion. Only in this manner can he obtain the representative opinion of the group.

THE DIGNITY OF THE CHAIRMAN

The chairman holds a dignified position. Don't spoil it by treating the matter too lightly. Don't exchange banter with the audience. Make everyone realise that you will not stand for any nonsense—and that includes hecklers. See that there is respect for the chair.

You are there to guide—to control. You are there to see that the right of free speech is maintained.

You are upholding a great tradition—see that you uphold it in a right and proper manner.

CHAPTER XVIII

On Lecturing

ABOUT six lectures a day, thirty lectures a week, for fifty-two weeks in the year . . . That's quite a lot of lecturing, but it is undertaken by my colleagues and myself and we all thoroughly enjoy it.

Lecturing is very similar to public speaking. The dictionary definition of a lecture is: *A lesson or period of instruction.* Public speakers, as a rule, don't instruct—they inform, but they rarely teach. A lecturer teaches.

You may like to know how we prepare a lecture from the beginning. Let us start with the assumption that we are seeking a lecturer for a specific subject. Here are the main attributes we would expect him to possess:

A complete knowledge of the subject he is to teach.
Sincerity.
A pleasant voice (accents don't matter at all).
No platform mannerisms.

Bernard Shaw once said: *He who can, does. He who cannot, teaches.* This may apply to some public speakers, but it should certainly not apply to lecturers. A public speaker, without knowing a great deal about a subject, can usually obtain sufficient information to enable him to make a short speech about it.

Not so the lecturer. He should be greatly experienced and must know much more about his subject than the students he is to teach. Not only must he know it thoroughly, but he must enjoy imparting his knowledge to others, otherwise he cannot have enthusiasm, and a lecture is not worth listening to unless it is presented enthusiastically.

Having selected our lecturer we must decide on the type of lecture he is best able to give. We should do much the same as we advised you to do when building up your speech. When I refer to 'we', I mean the group of lecturers, because we all take an interest in each other's talks.

We should spend several days thinking, studying the subject and asking questions, until each one of us had collected a number of facts. A meeting would then be called, and all the facts would be discussed. The lecturer himself would have authority to veto anything which he did not feel he could include confidently and enthusiastically. At the end of the discussion we should have a complete set of facts around which to build the talk for the lecturer. He would then be asked to develop his lecture utilising these facts.

Rehearsals

As soon as our lecturer felt confident that he had made sufficient progress with his talk, he would rehearse it in front of the group. There would be no interruptions during his lecture, and no comments after it. We should all think around it for a few days, and then there would be a second rehearsal. At its conclusion we should discuss the various points brought out by the lecturer. We should try to help improve his presentation. Analogies would be suggested, quotations, stories, in fact all the things we had thought of during the interval between the two rehearsals.

At a third rehearsal the lecturer would present an amended talk based on the final decisions of the group discussion. But that would not end the rehearsals. Next there would have to be a rehearsal to include demonstrations, the use of visual aids, and audience participation.

Audience Participation

If it is possible for a lecturer to let his audience participate in some way during his lectures, then he will hold their interest, and be a better teacher. If members of the audience can be invited to carry out demonstrations on the platform it will help considerably.

We learn quickly when we are allowed to *do the things that we are being taught.*

VISUAL AIDS

We believe that no lecturer should talk for any length of time without using some form of visual aid. It is difficult for anyone to listen continuously, even to the finest lecturer, without a break.

Here are some visual aids we can recommend:

1. *Something That Moves*

    The audience is always interested in something that moves. Can anything be supplied which would line up with the lecturer's talk? Could he use a film, or a moving sign?

2. *A Magnetic Board*

    Can he use a magnetic board? This is always an effective visual aid.

    Colour should be used whenever possible.

3. A Blackboard

A good many lecturers use a blackboard, but it has so many disadvantages. Writing becomes illegible after the board has been sponged down several times. It is far better to use large sheets of white paper clamped together by two pieces of wood, which can be affixed to a standard easel. A black or coloured crayon can be used and the paper can be torn off and discarded as each sheet is finished.

4. Working Models

These will always interest the audience, and should be used whenever possible.

Gradually the lecture is taking form. The length of the talk has been cut down; visual aids have been included. Next we ask ourselves if charts will be effective.

CHARTS

Linen Sheets

We use linen sheets for our charts. We find that they are easier to handle than large cards, because we use several of them, and it is easy for the lecturer to turn them over as he finishes with each one.

If it is not possible to use linen sheets, then sheets of white paper, prepared before the lecture commences, make a good substitute.

The Size

The charts we use are 3 ft. by 2 ft. 6 in. These can be seen from any part of the room, and we make sure that the printing on them is legible.

Is It Clear?

Make certain that the message on the chart can be understood. If the lecturer has first to explain what the chart is all about, then the chart cannot be worth having. It should speak for itself, and it can only do this if it is not overcrowded with words, figures, drawings, etc.

The fewer points you have on each chart the better.

Illustrations

We try to illustrate our charts if we can. Illustrations always arouse interest.

DRESS REHEARSAL

Now we come to our dress rehearsal. The lecturer speaks, uses his visual aids, uses his charts. He is carefully timed throughout his speech, so that subsequently he will know, merely by glancing at his watch, whether he is ahead of time or behind time.

And so the lecture is born.

YOU

Why have I given you this information on how we prepare our lectures? Because I want to impress upon you the great care that has to be taken with them.

You may not be able to have a group with which to discuss your plans, but you can enlist the help of your friends and your family, and you can go through a similar procedure to that which we adopt. You can rehearse time and time again.

Nothing must be left to chance, for when nothing is left to chance, the lecture will go like clockwork. As well as complying with the dictionary definition: *A lesson or period of instruction*, it will also be interesting and enjoyable.

CHAPTER XIX

Public Speaking Guides

THE next time you attend a meeting to listen to a speaker, count the number of times your attention is distracted from the speech because of some incident on the platform. Audiences listening to *you* will be equally distracted if you speak from a platform crowded with members of a committee, delegates, speakers or other officials. One talks to another; one glances at his watch; one makes notes . . .

Whenever, therefore, you make a speech from a platform, try to have that platform to yourself. Enlightened organisers and chairmen will arrange this for you. Otherwise, a word in the ear of the secretary may bring about the desired result.

No Empty Spaces

If there are empty chairs at the back of the hall it matters little. It matters a great deal, however, if the back rows are full and the front rows remain half-empty. This handicaps a speaker from the start. He feels that he is talking to chairs and not to human beings.

See that the stewards fill the front rows before you speak. If this cannot be arranged, gather the audience together yourself.

Check

Here are some last-minute check points:

    1. Check the acoustics. If there are pillars in the

room, or the room is of an awkward shape—
T-shaped, for example—you will know that
you have to raise your voice when speaking.

If there is an echo, you will have to speak
slowly and deliberately.

2. Check the lighting, so as to be sure of being
able to read your notes.

3. Have the organisers provided you with a table
or lectern or a desk? If so, is it of the correct
height? If nothing has been provided, see that
something is done about it, otherwise you will
have to hold your notes in your hand.

4. If you are using visual aids or props, see that
they are all ready and in position before the
meeting commences.

Don't Compete

Don't compete with noises-off or disturbances
caused by waiters. Ask a steward to position himself
near one of the exits, so that he will be able to deal
with any noise immediately it starts. It might be caused
by hotel staff shouting to each other, plates being
rattled in a kitchen, etc.

See that instructions are given to waiters to take
their orders from the guests before you begin to speak.
They should leave the room then, until you have
finished speaking.

The Table Plan

Ask the organisers to avoid having a U-shaped table
if possible. If not, you will be talking most of the time
to an expanse of carpet.

Toasts

Here are some general rules on toasts:

1. *The Loyal Toast.* This does not need a speech. You merely rise and say:

> "Gentlemen (or ladies and gentlemen), the Queen!"

If there are persons of distinction present, then the toast will be:

> "Your Royal Highness (if a Prince of the blood royal is present), Mr. Chairman (or my Lord Chairman if he is a peer, or Sir John, etc., if he is a knight), my Lords, ladies and gentlemen: The Queen!"

2. If you are to propose a toast, for example, to *The Company* you will couple with it the name of the person who is to reply.

3. If you are to reply to a toast, you may have to add notes to your Confidence Cards. The proposer of the toast may make some unexpected remarks which call for a response on your part.

Microphones

If you are going to use a microphone, check it to see that it is working correctly before your speech commences, and then arrange for a steward to make a further check just before you speak. Two checks are better than one.

If, while you are speaking, you don't think the loud-speaker system is operating, stop speaking until the fault has been remedied. There is little sense in continuing to speak when, perhaps, fifty per cent of the audience cannot hear what you are saying.

Here are some more rules for microphone users:

1. Do not touch it when you are speaking. A slight tap on a microphone may mean a loud bang to the audience.

2. Do not stand too close to the microphone. There is no need for this with modern sensitive equipment.

3. Do not talk to the microphone. Address your remarks to the audience. They want to look at you, and you should look at them.

4. Lower or raise the microphone so as to avoid its hiding your face. It is disconcerting for an audience to have to watch a speaker's ears and a part of his head, because the microphone is hiding the rest of his features.

A Professional Technique

Always use the pause. Professional speakers pause frequently during their speech. That's good showmanship.

Tape Recorders

With the innovation of tape recorders the lot of the tyro public speaker has become easier. If you have such a recorder you will find it useful to record your speeches in advance. You can then listen carefully to see that your interest points are well spaced out. You can hear whether those inflections of your voice are right, note the changes of pace in your speech, and so on.

Give It a Title

Give your speech a title, even if it is not necessary to do so. This will help you to emphasise in your own mind the major point that you are trying to drive home in your speech.

Avoid Stock Phrases

It is sometimes difficult to avoid one of the standard phrases which we all use on occasion, but it is far better to try to be original. Here are some of the phrases which you might do well to avoid :

> Last but not least . . .
> Quick as lightning . . .
> Silent as the Sphinx . . .
> Look with pride . . .
> No stone unturned . . .
> Call to mind . . .
> Slow but sure . . .
> The long and short of it .
> By and large . . .
> Reached a milestone . . .
> Stood the test of time . . .
> If I may say so . . .
> In my humble opinion . . .
> A man in a million . . .

The Notebook

To be a successful speaker you should possess a speaker's notebook, as well as a card-index system. Each day you will find something interesting to add to your notebook. An item in your daily newspaper—an anecdote from a magazine—an extract from a book—

an epigram used during a conversation—a human interest story told on the radio—all can be recorded. In the evening, transfer these notes to your cards. Have different sets of cards for anecdotes, analogies, humorous stories, quotations, and so on. Keep an index for your cards, so that when you are about to prepare a speech you can find what you want quickly and easily.

COURAGE

A speaker must have courage—courage to face an antagonistic audience—courage to voice his convictions—courage to use his talents to speak for those unable to speak for themselves—courage to stand on his two feet and speak when he doesn't feel like speaking—courage never to let the audience down, the show must always go on.

This is what Sydney Smith had to say about *courage*:

> *A great deal of talent is lost in the world for want of a little courage. Every day sends to their graves obscure men whom timidity prevented from making a first effort; who, if they could have been induced to begin, would in all probability have gone great lengths in the career of fame. The fact is, that to do anything in the world worth doing, we must not stand back shivering and thinking of the cold and danger, but jump in and scramble through as well as we can. It will not do to be perpetually calculating risks and adjusting nice chances; it did very well before the Flood, when a man would consult his friends upon an intended publication for a hundred and fifty years, and live to see his success afterwards; but at*

present, a man waits, and doubts, and consults his brother, and his particular friends, till one day he finds he is sixty years old and that he has lost so much time in consulting cousins and friends that he has no more time to follow their advice.

Take the advice given to you in this book— and may you have many happy years as a SUCCESSFUL SPEAKER.

CHAPTER XX

A Discussion

"How," asked George, "are you going to end the book?"

"What do you mean?" I answered. "I've already ended it by quoting Sydney Smith. Because I didn't pad the book with speech after speech, and quotation after quotation, I was surely entitled to do that."

"Of course," said George. "I'm not arguing about that. But I do feel that you should conclude the book with a check-up chart."

"For what reason?" I asked. "Check-up charts don't help. They only prove that we are perfect to ourselves. Only yesterday you discovered that you are the perfect husband, because you filled in a check-up chart in the paper."

"And you proved that you were the perfect gourmet in the same way."

"Then," I asked, "what's the use of charts?"

"I just like them!" George hesitated for a few minutes, then he stood up and said, "I've got it! I have a brilliant idea!"

I eyed him warily. I've had some of his brilliant ideas before. Usually they mean that he's just thought of another way of making me work harder.

"Well?" I queried.

"Use one of the standard closes for a speech. That would be perfect."

"How do you mean?" I did not sound enthusiastic.

"The summary close—obviously! List all the major

points, one after the other: First they must learn to relax; then study human relations; next they must master the *does-it-apply-to-me* technique; one-minute speeches must be followed by a study of words; the speech-building formula . . ."

"Just a minute!" I exploded. "If I do all that, a possible buyer of the book may look at the end of it first and decide that he doesn't need to buy it."

"And what makes you think," said George unkindly, "that anyone is going to buy the book?"

That started a short discussion. We lit cigarettes and talked again about closing techniques.

"You know," said George, "you could finish with a question close. Ask a question, and leave it at that. For example:

> "Did you build up a speech on the Welfare State, or did you leave it over to do later? The man who leaves things over never succeeds."

I shook my head. "Not too keen," I said, "although it's true enough."

"You'd have been keen all right if you'd thought of it," said George.

"I'm not disputing that it's excellent advice. It just isn't strong enough for a close. Now I think a good poetic close might be the answer."

"And that can only mean," said George, "that you are going to recite:

> "Somebody said it couldn't be done, but he with a chuckle replied
> "That maybe it couldn't, but he would be one who wouldn't say so till he'd tried;

"So he buckled right in with a trace of a grin on his
    face, if he worried he hid it.
"He started to sing as he tackled the thing that
    couldn't be done—AND HE DID IT."

"What's wrong with that?" I asked, when he had
finished his recitation. "It sums everything up, doesn't
it? So many would-be speakers are put off by well-
meaning friends, whereas if they'd only buckle right in
—why, they'd do it."

"I agree," said my brother. "But it isn't highbrow
enough. Surely you'd be better to use a strong quotation. As you have driven home human relations all the
way through the book, why not quote Lord Chester-
field:

"*The manner of your speaking is full important as
the matter, as more people have ears to be tickled than
understandings to judge.*"

"No," I said, "that wouldn't be a high note. And
in any event, human relations is not more important
than the subject matter of a speech—they are both
equally important."

"I have it!" said George. "This time I really have
it. A concession close! Invite the reader to write to you
if he needs help."

"They do that without invitation. That wouldn't be
a concession. Don't you think, George," I went on,
"that a good close would be the chairman's remarks
after we had both made a speech at that farewell
dinner given to us when we left New York? That
would be a nice conclusion."

"Yes," said George, "it would."

And these are the words the chairman used:

> *It's good to know the work you are doing in Great Britain. Your leaders of industry have remained silent too long. We want to hear what they have to say for themselves. We'd like them to come over and talk to us. You may say that there's no need for them to sell old England, but they can tell us what you are doing, because the more we understand you, the more we like you. Understanding is the basis of mutual friendship . . .*

AND ONE WAY TO ACHIEVE THAT
UNDERSTANDING IS BY
PUBLIC SPEAKING.

The
TACK ORGANISATION

is the largest training organisation of its kind in the world. It has twelve thousand client companies in the United Kingdom including many leading names in industry and commerce. Companies in the TACK group market products and services through every type of outlet and provide the up-to-date practical experience on which all training is based.

This practically, together with highly professional teaching methods, has largely accounted for the success and growth of the Training Division, which offers these courses:

■ FINANCE
Finance for the Senior Executive
Introduction to Finance for Managers
Cash Collection and Credit Control
Introduction to International Commerce

■ MANAGEMENT AND SUPERVISORY
Leadership in Senior Management
The Multi-Discipline Manager
Executive Development
Communication and Negotiation Skills
   for Managers
Motivational Leadership
Effective Supervision
Effective Supervision – Part 2
Effective Office Management
Effective Office Management – Part 2
Profitable Time Management
Executive Decision Making
Recruitment Interviewing and
   Selection
Performance Appraisal

■ COMMUNICATION
Effective Speaking
Effective Report Writing
Better Letter Writing
Better Use of the Telephone

■ SALES
Sales Training
Sales Training – Part 2
Selling to Industry
Selling to Industry – Part 2
Professional Sales Development
Profitable Negotiating
Professional Telephone Selling
Dealing with Customers by Telephone
Successful Territory Management
Selling to Wholesalers and Retailers
Selling Financial Services
Better Selling through Financial
   Awareness

■ MARKETING AND SALES MANAGEMENT
Field Sales Management
Field Sales Management - Part 2
Profitable Sales Management
Introduction to Marketing

■ SPECIALIST TRAINING
Caring for the Customer
Customer Relations for Service
   Engineers
The Executive Secretary
Introduction to Microcomputers
Training the Trainer

In-Company Training is provided in all these areas, specially designed to suit specific client requirements.

Open Courses are run regularly on most of the above topics, with mixed attendance by client companies from all areas of industry and commerce.

THE TACK ORGANISATION
LONGMOORE STREET LONDON SW1V 1JJ
Telephone 01-834-5001

Other books written by

ALFRED TACK

Building, Training and Motivating a Sales Force

Using the Tack Interviewing and Selection formula, followed by
Tack Training and Motivation Techniques this book shows how to
build a highly efficient sales force.
   The contents include:
      Devising a complete sales training course
      Training the trainer courses
      Refresher and development courses
      Motivating salesmen by performance appraisal

Executive Development

Based on the Tack Executive Development Course this book covers:
      Situation adaptable leadership
      Managing Conflict
      Time Management and communication
      Self-development, change and stress
      Decision-making, problem-solving.

How to Increase Sales to Industry

Shows Salesmen the way success can be achieved. Whether they are
negotiating a large contract or seeking repeat business. The book is
based on the world-famous Tack Course Selling to Industry.

How to Increase Sales by Telephone

Thousands of pounds worth of business are lost every day by poor telephone technique.

Based on the Tack Telephone Selling Course this book covers in detail every aspect of telephone usage, including:
>   Planning telephone presentation
>   Dealing with difficult customers
>   Reviving inactive accounts, promoting sales

How to Succeed in Selling

This is the standard book for The Tack Sales Courses, based on the practical experiences of salesmen.

A practical work which is indispensible reading for salesmen, young and old, for those at the beginning of their careers, and for well-established salesmen seeking fresh ideas to invigorate their sales techniques

Marketing: The Sales Manager's Role

This book defines the Sales Manager's Role and examines in detail the responsibilities. It guides and advises on all aspects of the Sales Manager's work covering:
>   Long range planning, market research
>   Budgeting, forecasting, sales costs
>   Public relations, advertising
>   Stimulation and encouragement of sales force

1000 Ways to Increase Your Sales

The title is self-explanatory, the contents include:
>   One certain way to increase sales
>   Proven Sales Techniques
>   How to make people want to buy from you
>   The right way to handle objections
>   Fifty ways to chasing more orders
>   How to handle every type of buyer

Sell Better, Live Better
One of the most original books on salesmanship. This is a series of
articles on how to overcome the difficulty of maintaining friendship
and imparting information to customer and salesman alike.

  Also includied are letters received from readers, telling how Alfred
Tack has helped them to succeed in life.

Published by

CEDAR BOOKS
an imprint of
William Heinemann Ltd

Other CEDAR titles ...

* New in 1988